CUTAWAY
TRUCKS

JON KIRKWOOD

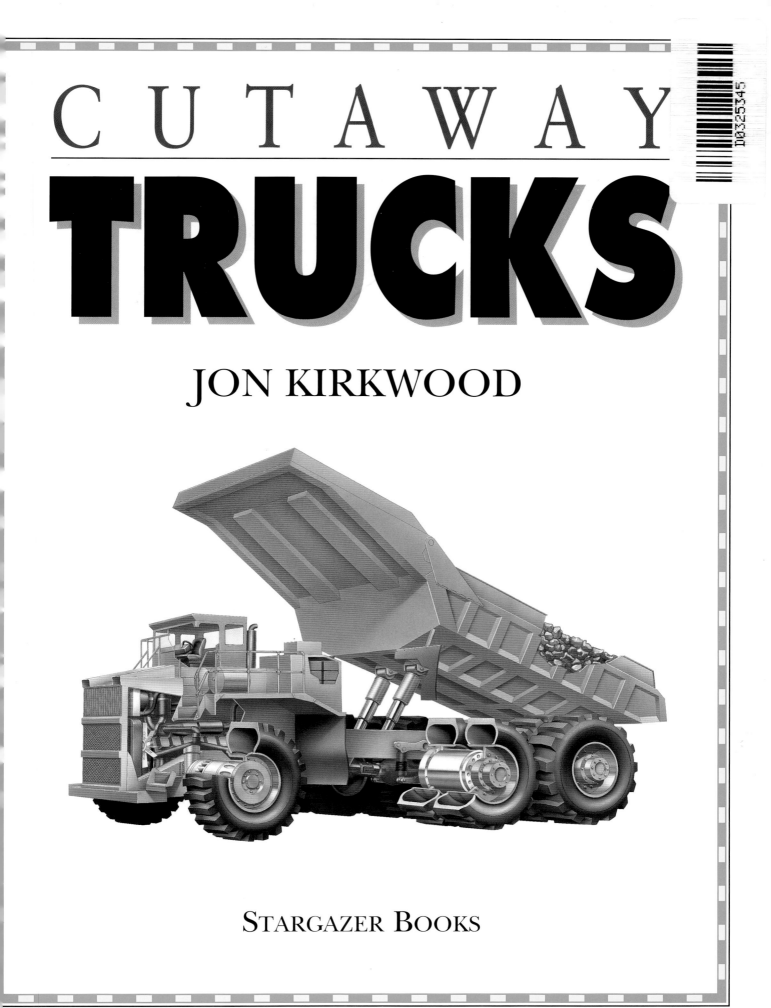

STARGAZER BOOKS

Designed and
produced by
Aladdin Books Ltd

Editor
Jon Richards
Consultant
Steve Allman
Design
David West Children's
Book Design
Designer
Robert Perry
Illustrators
Simon Tegg & Graham White
Picture Research
Brooks Krikler Research

CONTENTS

INTRODUCTION

Trucks are vital for our way of life. They carry large loads from place to place. Trucks with cranes also let us lift objects high into the air with the greatest of ease. There are trucks for other important jobs. They can mix concrete, carry logs, dig holes, race each other at high speeds, do stunts, and even swim rivers.

TRACTOR UNIT

The front parts of trucks that bend in the middle are called tractor units. Drivers sit inside the cabs at the front of the tractor units. From here, they can steer the trucks along the road. Some cabs may even have beds in the back (*see* pages 16-17)!

Beneath or in front of the cab is the engine. This needs to be very powerful to drive the tractor unit and pull its load. This engine is as strong as the engines from ten small cars!

Trailer link
Behind the cab is a device that links the tractor unit to a trailer. This special link lets the articulated truck bend in the middle. The truck can then turn very tight corners.

Fuel tank
The fuel tank contains the fuel for the tractor unit's engine.

Wheels
A tractor unit has two or more sets of wheels. The front set steers the tractor unit. The rear sets push the tractor unit along and carry the weight of the trailer.

Exhaust
Fumes from the engine are carried away by the exhaust pipe.

Horn
A loud horn warns other drivers that the tractor unit is nearby.

Engine
Sometimes a fault might occur in the engine. The whole cab is then tilted forward to let the mechanic reach the engine and fix it.

Trucks come in all

Funnel

Boiler

Wheel

Steering wheel

Steam-powered truck

Early trucks (*above*) used steam engines instead of diesel engines. Water was heated in a boiler to make steam that gave the power to drive the truck.

Vans or SUVs

Some of the most popular vehicles are vans or SUVs (right). They can be used to carry small loads as well as people.

shapes and sizes.

One-piece trucks

Some trucks come in one piece (*below*). At the front of the truck is the cab where the driver sits. Behind this, the truck is fitted with one type of body unit. This could be a rubbish compactor, a crane, or a container.

Container

Articulated trucks

Some trucks have trailers that are pulled by a tractor unit. Between the tractor unit and the trailer is a special device that allows the truck to bend. These trucks are called articulated trucks. Sometimes, a tractor unit may pull more than one trailer (*right*).

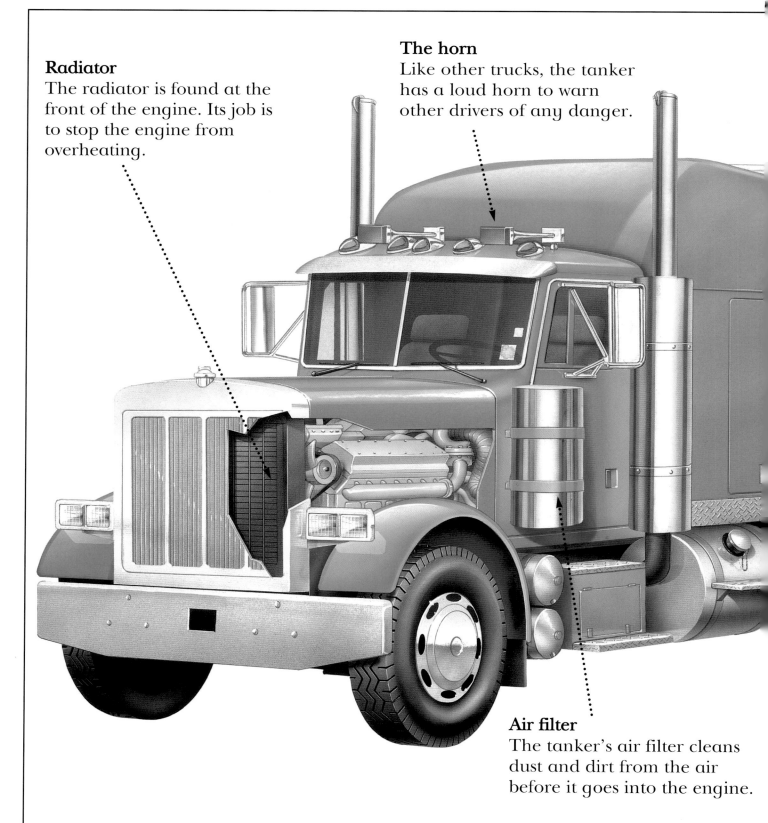

Radiator
The radiator is found at the front of the engine. Its job is to stop the engine from overheating.

The horn
Like other trucks, the tanker has a loud horn to warn other drivers of any danger.

Air filter
The tanker's air filter cleans dust and dirt from the air before it goes into the engine.

TANKER

Tankers pull special types of trailers. These trailers are designed to carry liquids, such as gasoline and milk.

Fuel in
Fuel is put into the tanker through hatches on the top of the trailer.

Double skin
The trailer is made from two layers of tough metal. These stop it from splitting open if there is an accident.

Fuel out
Fuel comes out of the tanker through pipes under the trailer.

A fuel tanker is filled with either gasoline or diesel at the storage depot. The tanker then carries its load to gas stations.

Here the fuel is pumped out of the tanker and into storage tanks. These storage tanks are usually kept underground.

Trailers are used to

Low-loader

A truck that can bend between the trailer and the tractor unit is called an articulated truck. Sometimes, they may be fitted with a very low trailer, called a low-loader. These are designed to carry very heavy or very large loads (*above* and *right*).

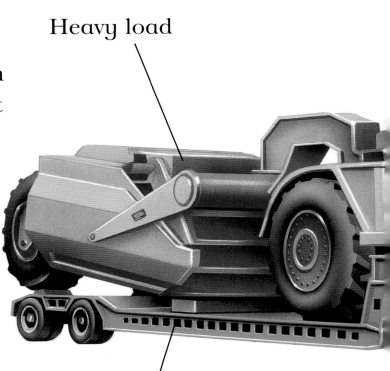

Heavy load

Low trailer

Logging truck

Some articulated trucks carry logs (*left*). Here, sets of wheels are fixed to either end of the logs. The logs and wheels together act as a trailer.

carry heavy loads.

More than one

To carry a lot of cargo, more than one trailer may be used, as with a road-train. These make the truck very long (*right*).

Cab

Car transporter

Some trailers are made to carry cars. These trailers have two or even three decks. This means that one truck and trailer can carry up to eleven cars at a time (*below*).

Cab

The driver sits in a cab that is tiny compared to the rest of the truck. To get to the cab the driver has to climb up a ladder.

Engine and fuel tank

The engine that drives a dump truck needs to be very powerful. Its fuel tank holds enough to fill 50 bathtubs!

Pistons

Two pistons raise the front of the dump truck's hopper.

Hopper

Some dump trucks can carry loads that weigh as much as 70 elephants. When it is tipping out its load, the top of the hopper can reach as high as a five-story building!

Wheels

This dump truck has huge wheels. Each one is more than the height of two adults!

DUMP TRUCK

Quarries and mines are places where massive amounts of rock are dug from the ground by enormous digging machines called excavators. Huge dump trucks are needed to carry the rocks away. The excavators empty the rocks into a container at the back of the dump truck. This container is called the hopper. The truck then drives to where the load is to be dumped. When it reaches the site, two pistons push the front of the hopper up. The rocks then simply slide out of the back of the hopper.

13

Trucks do a lot of

Concrete mixer

Concrete is carried to a building site in a concrete mixer (*below*). This has a mixing drum on the back that turns slowly to mix the concrete. When it reaches the site, concrete is poured out through the delivery chute.

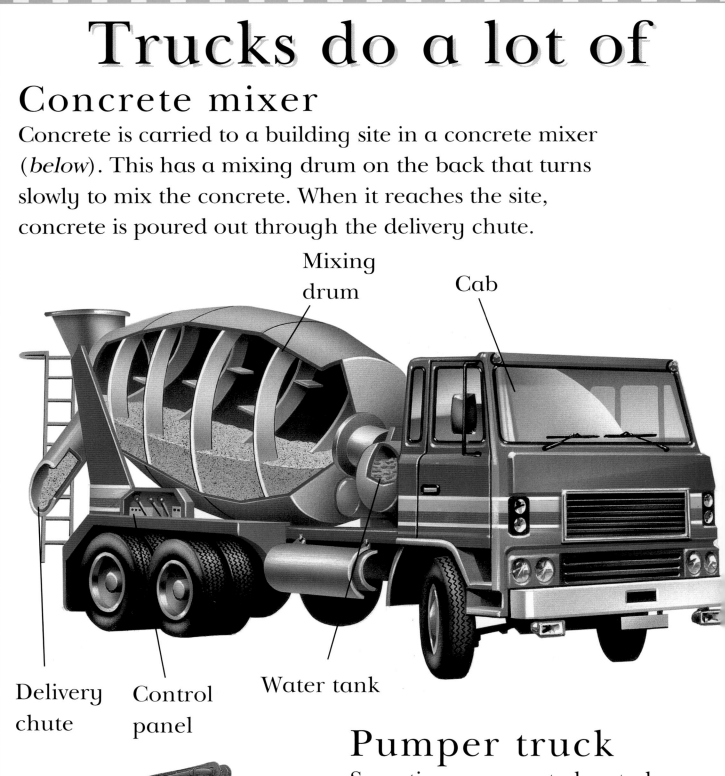

Mixing drum

Cab

Delivery chute

Control panel

Water tank

Pumper truck

Sometimes, concrete has to be pumped up to high places from a concrete mixer. When this happens a special pumper truck (*left*) is used.

14

jobs on building sites.

Tipper truck

A tipper truck (*left*) carries loads or containers. When the truck reaches the site where the cargo is needed, the rear tilts up and the cargo slides off.

Loader

Loaders (*right*) are fitted with huge shovels on the front. They are used to scoop up piles of rocks and earth and dump them in the back of other trucks.

Scraper

These large trucks (*left*) are used to move large amounts of earth. Underneath the truck is a large blade that skims along the ground, digging up the top layer of the soil.

Inside the cab

Driving a truck is a tough job to do. Truck drivers may spend many hours on the road. To make their lives as easy as possible, trucks are built with many of the comforts of home (*right*).

Top bunk

Curtains

Double bed

Closet

Instrument panel

The instrument panels on the dashboard (*left*) give the driver information about the truck. The panel includes dials showing speed, the distance traveled, engine temperature, and fuel level.

be a truck driver.

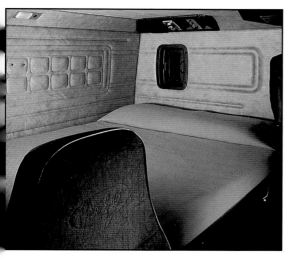

Living area

In some cabs there are living quarters for the driver to use. There may be a bed (*left*) and washing facilities including a shower. Some trucks have a small kitchen with a refrigerator, and a relaxation area, perhaps with a desk for doing paperwork.

Suspension

A truck's wheels are fitted with springs and pistons (*right*). These make the ride very smooth for the driver.

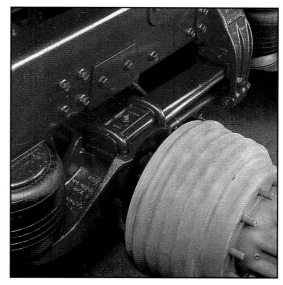

Smooth body

The shape of a tractor unit is built to be smooth (*left*). This helps it slip through the air as easily as possible. As a result, the truck uses less fuel, and can carry loads farther.

Crane
The arm of the crane can stretch. When it is fully extended, it can reach out over a third of a soccer field.

Lifting block
Heavy loads are attached to a hook on the end of the lifting block. They are then lifted to where they are wanted.

TRUCK CRANE

Once the truck has arrived at the site the driver puts down the stabilizers before climbing into the crane cab.

Crane cab

The driver operates the crane from here. There are levers to turn the crane around and move the end up and down.

Turntable

The base of the crane is attached to a turntable. This can turn the crane around in a complete circle.

Stabilizer

There are four of these. They stop the truck from falling over when it lifts heavy objects.

Wheels

There are four sets of twin wheels to carry the heavy load. There are also two wheels to steer with at the front.

Once in the cab the driver can operate the crane. A telescopic arm moves the crane in and out. A piston moves the arm up and down. The truck crane has two diesel engines. One is used to power the truck while the other powers the crane.

Trucks can pick up

Fork lift truck

A fork lift truck has two forks at the front. These forks are placed under a load to lift it. The strongest fork lift trucks can lift a load that weighs as much as 15 elephants.

Lifting forks

Engine

Cherry picker

A cherry-picker truck (*left*) has a platform at the end of an arm. This arm stretches up to reach high above the ground. The whole truck is kept steady by four stabilizers (*see* page 19).

big and small loads.

Heavy-lift crane

When very large loads need lifting, a heavy-lift crane (*right*) is used. These huge trucks can have ten sets of wheels. The huge arm of the crane can stretch almost the length of a soccer field. As with a smaller truck crane (*see* pages 18-19), this crane uses stabilizers to keep it steady.

This enormous crane (below) weighs as much as a blue whale.

Rear wheels

SWIMMING TRUCK

Some special trucks are able to swim across lakes and rivers. They are called amphibious trucks. When they travel over the ground, they are driven by their wheels, just like normal trucks. However, when they enter the water, propellers spin to push the amphibious truck along.

This amphibious truck (*right*) is used by the army to carry other vehicles across a river. It can also be used to build bridges across rivers. Several of these trucks swim alongside each other to form the bridge. They can build a bridge as long as a soccer field in only 20 minutes.

Engine
The engine is at the rear of the vehicle. It drives the vehicle over land and turns the propeller when it is "swimming."

Crane
There is a small crane mounted on the vehicle. This is used to lift the heavy parts of the bridge into place.

Ramps
The ramps are laid across the truck when it is being used as a bridge. They also carry the load when the truck is being used as a ferry.

Cab
When it drives over ground, the driver sits inside the cab. However, the cab is underwater when the truck is swimming. The driver then uses a set of controls on the roof at the back of the truck.

Some trucks don't

Armored vehicles

This armored car (*right*) weighed as much as five elephants! It was equipped with a gun and had armor to protect the soldiers inside. Armored trucks are used to carry equipment and soldiers around a battlefield.

Gun

Wheel

Armored body

Trucks on tracks

This truck (*left*) is used to carry out repairs on railroads. It is fitted with special wheels, called bogies, that allow the truck to drive along the rail tracks.

always drive on roads.

Desert trucks

Some trucks have to drive through the desert (*right*). To cope with the tough ground they need tough suspension (*see* page 17) and large tires.

Icy trucks

Trucks that drive over ice and snow use extra-wide wheels that are fitted with special snow tires (*below*). These tires give the truck extra grip and stop it from sliding about. They also stop the truck from sinking into the snow.

Cab
Cabs are equipped with special safety cages to protect the drivers. They also have safety harnesses to stop the drivers from being thrown around.

Engine
Racing trucks are equipped with very powerful engines. These can be twice as powerful as a normal tractor-unit engine!

Body work

Some racing trucks are fitted with extra body parts. These help the trucks drive faster by letting them move through the air as easily as possible.

RACING TRUCK

Racing trucks are tractor units that are altered to make them go faster. These trucks race each other around race tracks. They are equipped with more powerful engines, allowing them to go much faster than normal trucks. Lightweight materials are used throughout the truck to make it as light as possible. Even the glass of the windows and windshield is replaced. These new materials also have to be strong to protect the driver if there is a crash.

Brakes

Racing trucks have brakes that get very hot during racing. They are cooled with water to stop them from getting too hot.

Some other jobs

Tow truck

Sometimes a car or a truck breaks down and cannot drive any farther. When this happens a tow truck (*below*) will attach a hook to the vehicle and lift one end. The tow truck then pulls the broken vehicle to a garage where it can be fixed.

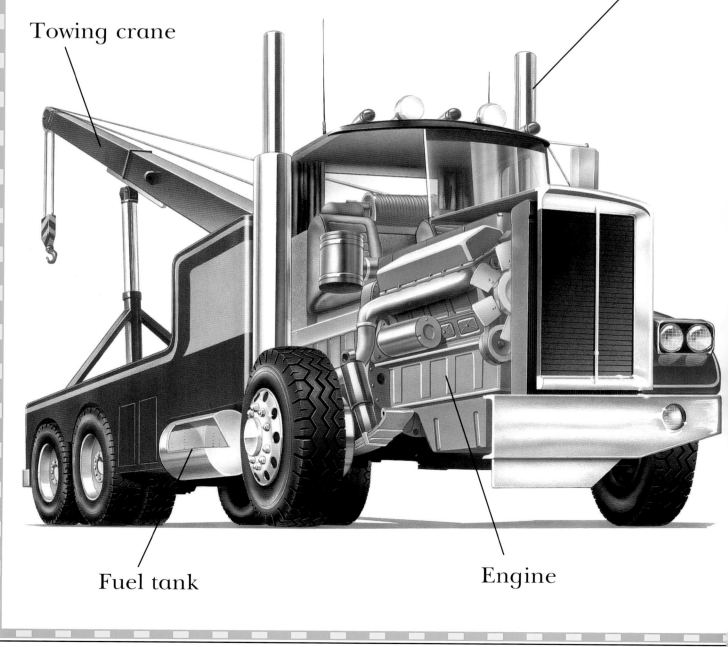

Exhaust

Towing crane

Fuel tank

Engine

that trucks do.

Racing team

These trucks (*right*) carry the cars and equipment for a motor racing team. At the end of the race, the trucks are loaded up and then driven off to the next event.

Fun trucks

Many trucks are altered to do special stunts. Some of them can do wheelies (*left*). Other trucks, called monster trucks, have huge wheels and crush other cars when they drive over them (*below*).

Fantastic Facts

- The first truck was built in 1769 by the Frenchman Nicolas-Joseph Cugnot. It was powered by steam and was built to pull cannons into battle. However, it lost control during testing and was never used again.

- The longest truck in the world was an Australian road-train. Pulling five trailers, this truck was as long as 15 cars, weighed as much as 150 cars, and had 110 wheels!

- The most powerful tow truck in the world is called the "Hulk." It can pull the weight of two blue whales!

- The fastest truck in the world is powered by three jet-fighter engines and can drive at 256 mph (412 km/h)!

Glossary

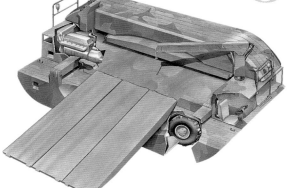

Amphibious truck
A road truck that can also swim. Its engine drives both the wheels and a propeller.

Articulated truck
A truck that comes in two or more parts. At the front is the tractor unit that pulls one or more trailers.

Bogies
These are special wheels that are built to run on rail tracks.

Cherry picker
A truck that has a platform on the end of an arm. This arm can extend, lifting the platform to high places.

Diesel
A type of fuel that is used in truck and car engines.

Suspension
A system of springs and other devices that smooth the ride of a truck.

Tractor unit
The front part of an articulated truck. The driver sits in the tractor unit to drive the truck. It also contains the engine.

Trailer
Towed behind a truck or tractor unit, the trailer is the part that carries the load or cargo.

Index

PHOTO CREDITS
Abbreviations: t-top, m-middle, b-bottom, r-right, l-left, c-center.
Pages 4, 13, 15m – Roger Vlitos. 6 – Zefa. 7t – Foden/Paccar.
7b, 10b, 11t, 14, 15t, 16, 17t & m – Peterbilt/Paccar. 8, 15b, 18 –
Spectrum Colour Library. 10t – Caterpillar. 11b, 25t, 27,
29m – Eye Ubiquitous. 17b – Kenworth Truck
Company. 20, 21 both, 24 – Liebherr. 22 – EWK.
25b – James Davis Travel Photography.
29t – Renault. 29b – Frank Spooner Pictures.

LOOK INSIDE MACHINES

DIGGERS

JON RICHARDS

Franklin Watts
London • Sydney

© Aladdin Books Ltd

*Designed and
produced by*
Aladdin Books Ltd

Editor
Michael Flaherty

Consultant
Steve Allman
Design
David West
Children's Book Design
Designer
Simon Morse
Illustrators
Simon Tegg & Ross Watton
Picture Research
Brooks Krikler Research

CONTENTS

INTRODUCTION

Construction machines can be found wherever any building work is being done, from putting up small houses to laying long roads. Over the years, these mighty machines have replaced the work of hundreds of people. Today, enormous shovels can gouge huge holes in the ground, boring machines can dig long tunnels deep underground, and excavators can pull down tall buildings.

Front bucket

The front of the bucket is hinged so that the rubble can be easily dropped into a waiting truck. The bucket on this backhoe loader can lift nearly 3 tons of rock.

Engine power

The engine provides all the power to drive the backhoe loader, including raising the front bucket with a load of rubble and moving the backhoe to dig.

Chunky tires

The backhoe loader has large, chunky tires to drive over rough ground.

Backhoe
At full stretch, the backhoe can reach out, or down, as far as the height of three adults lying head to toe. It is moved by controls at the back of the driver's cab.

BACKHOE LOADER

This unusual-looking machine is possibly the most useful digger on any building site. It has tools fitted to its front and to its back. On the front is a huge scoop, or bucket, that can be used to scoop up rubble. On the back is a movable arm, called a backhoe. This can be used to dig trenches or pull down buildings. It can also be fitted with different tools to do other jobs, such as a pneumatic drill (*see* page 18) and a mechanical claw.

Stabilizers
These special arms reach out to take the weight off the back wheels and to provide a steady platform when the backhoe is being used.

Diggers can come in

Foundation piles

When a tall building is being put up, it needs very deep foundations so it won't sink into the ground. Special cranes fitted with huge drill bits (*below*) dig holes into which the foundation piles are sunk.

Dredger

Not all diggers are used on land. A dredger (*above*) digs up mud from the bottom of the sea or a river. This stops the waterway from getting blocked.

all shapes and sizes.

Skid steer

This tiny building machine (*below*) is called a skid steer. It is very useful in small spaces because it can turn very tight corners.

Mini excavator

A mini excavator (*left*) is used where space is tight. With its small arm and bucket, it can dig very narrow trenches. The body of the excavator above the tracks can rotate in a full circle.

Engine

The engines used to power excavators need to be very strong. They can be nearly four times more powerful than the engine used to run a family car!

Cab

The cab is fitted with large glass screens to give the driver a good view of the excavator's arm.

In a spin

The top half of the excavator can spin around in a full circle. This lets the excavator dig up rubble from one side and drop it into a truck on the other side, without moving anywhere.

Caterpillar tracks

Caterpillar tracks have ridges to stop vehicles from slipping on soft or icy ground.

Hydraulic arm
The engine pumps fluids in and out of hydraulic rams on the excavator's arm. Inside these rams, the fluids push pistons in and out, moving the arm.

Hinged bucket
The bucket on an excavator is hinged, allowing it to be moved up and down, like your wrist.

Sharp teeth
As the arm pulls the bucket back, sharp metal teeth on the front of the bucket cut through the rubble and earth, scooping them up into the bucket.

EXCAVATOR

These mighty machines are seen on the largest building sites. They are used to dig the foundations beneath buildings, or to dig wide trenches. Their strong hydraulic arms (*see left*) are also used to pull down buildings, or they can be fitted with enormous claws to pick up heavy objects. Beneath the driver's cab are two large Caterpillar tracks. These spread the weight of the excavator over a larger area and stop it from sinking into soft ground. The largest excavators can weigh 80 tons — that's as much as 25 fully grown elephants!

Going, going, gone

Not all buildings can be demolished cheaply and quickly by machines. Very tall buildings may need dynamite to knock them down. Sticks of dynamite are put in places in the building where they will have most effect. When they explode, they cause the building to collapse (*right*). It takes a lot of skill to demolish a building without damaging surrounding buildings and spreading rubble everywhere!

to knock things down.

Bulldozer

When a building has been knocked down, the rubble has to be cleared away. Machines called bulldozers (*below*) are fitted with huge blades at the front. They push the debris to one side where it can be loaded into trucks.

Giant claw

The claw on the end of this machine (*right*) is used to pull down buildings. The driver's cab is fitted with bullet-proof glass to protect the operator.

Machines are used to

Tall cranes

The tallest cranes are put together in stages (*left*). They have long arms, or jibs, that sit on top of towers. Loads are lifted by cables and a hook from one end of the jib, while heavy weights on the other end stop the crane from falling over. This is called a tower crane.

Eye in the sky

The crane driver sits in a small cab at the top of the crane (*right*). From here, he or she controls where the crane's arm is pointing and how much cable is run out to lift or lower the load.

Into the air

Once they have been set up, cranes are used to lift almost any object into place. It could be a section of pipe (*left*), metal girder, some glass for a window, or a load of concrete.

Movable cranes

Not all cranes have to stay in one place. This mobile crane (*above* and *right*) is fitted onto a special truck. It has a long arm that can be extended and spun around.

Machines have made

Pick and shovel

Today, a single machine operated by one person can do the same work that used to take many people equipped with picks and shovels (*right*).

Full steam ahead

Before powerful internal combustion engines and electric motors were invented, building machines were powered by other means. This shovel (*above*) was powered by a steam engine.

building much easier.

Trench digging

Endless bucket trenchers use a series of small buckets on a belt. As this belt moves around, the buckets scoop out the earth to dig a trench. Bucket trenchers, like this one from 1901 (*right*), were used for many years, long before the invention of hydraulic arms (*see* page 9).

Steam press

Like the steam shovel (*see far left*), this roller (*left*) was powered by a steam engine. The roller's huge, heavy wheels were used to squash the surface of a road flat to make it smooth for vehicles to drive over.

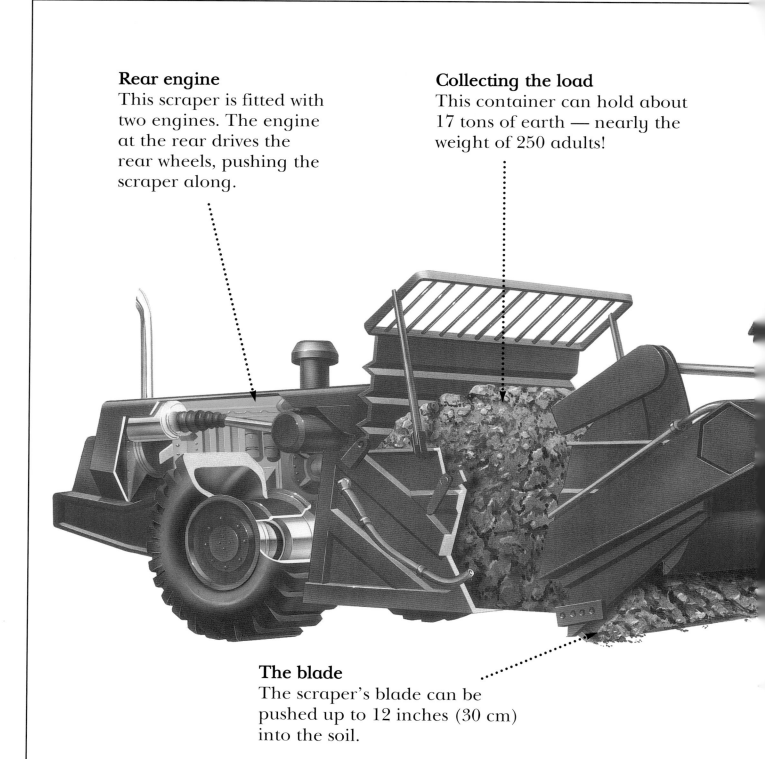

Rear engine
This scraper is fitted with two engines. The engine at the rear drives the rear wheels, pushing the scraper along.

Collecting the load
This container can hold about 17 tons of earth — nearly the weight of 250 adults!

The blade
The scraper's blade can be pushed up to 12 inches (30 cm) into the soil.

SCRAPER

This machine is used to scrape up layers of earth, preparing the ground for a road. It has a huge blade underneath that digs up

Hinged front

The tractor unit is linked to the rest of the scraper by a large hinge that bends to make turning easier.

Tractor unit

The front of the scraper, which contains one engine and the driver's cab, is called the tractor unit.

Powerful engines

In order to push and pull the scraper's blade through the ground, the engines need to be very powerful. Each engine of this scraper is as powerful as the engines from ten family cars!

the soil as the scraper drives forward. The soil is then collected in a huge container and carried to another site where the scraper can drop it. Sometimes, even the two engines in a scraper are not powerful enough and it may need to be pushed by another vehicle.

A lot of machines are

Digging it up

This backhoe loader has been fitted with a pneumatic drill (*left*). In this, air is squashed very hard, which forces a piston up and down. This piston smashes onto a tool, hammering it into the road.

Fine grades

A grader is fitted with an angled blade. As the grader drives along, this blade pushes the soil to one side to create the flat, even surface. This is called grading. It can also be used to create even slopes (*below*).

used to build a road.

Squashing it flat

After the asphalt has been laid (*see* pages 20-21), a roller (*left*) is used to squash it flat and make it smooth. The heaviest roller can weigh 35 tons — that's the same as 12 elephants!

Excavator

As well as demolishing buildings and digging trenches, excavators can be used to build roads (*left*). Their buckets can be used to move rubble and to grade soil to create an even surface.

Exhaust

As the engine burns fuel to work, it creates waste gases. These gases are carried out of the engine along a metal pipe called the exhaust.

Controls

On some road pavers, the steering wheel and other controls can be moved from one side of the paver to the other. This lets the driver keep a close eye on either side of the road.

Hopper

Dump trucks empty the hot asphalt into this large hopper at the front of the road paver.

Conveyor belt

This conveyor belt carries the asphalt from the hopper to the rear of the road paver.

Hotplates

Once the asphalt has been spread over the road, special heated plates, called soleplates, flatten and smooth the asphalt out. Sometimes, these soleplates can be extended so the paver can lay a wider road.

ROAD PAVER

Once a pathway has been dug for a road, the road's foundations are built by putting down layers of materials. The final layer is built by a road paver. This noisy, smelly machine moves forward slowly, spreading a thin layer of asphalt. This is a black, sticky substance that is mixed with stones. It can be squashed and shaped when it is hot and is rolled flat by a roller (*see* page 19) to make it smooth. When it cools, it sets hard enough to withstand heavy traffic. A paver is also used to replace old or damaged asphalt.

Giant corkscrew

At the back of the road paver is a large screw called an auger. This auger spins slowly, spreading the asphalt evenly across the road.

Massive machines

Wheel and bucket

This enormous machine (*below*) is used in huge opencast mines. It is fitted with a massive wheel ringed with buckets. It is called a bucket-wheel excavator. The huge wheel at the front of the excavator spins around, and the buckets gouge out earth.

Life's a drag

This massive digging machine (*left*) is called a drag-line excavator. It throws out an enormous bucket on the end of a cable and then drags it back over the surface. As it is dragged back, sharp metal teeth on the front of the bucket scrape up the earth.

Massive buckets

The buckets on a mining excavator need to be big (*right*). The largest buckets are wide enough to hold two family cars!

Strong arm

The hydraulic arm of a mining shovel has to be strong enough to lift the bucket and a full load of rock. In some cases this load can weigh as much as five adult elephants!

Bucket

The tip of the bucket has sharp, strong teeth to break up the rock. The bottom of the bucket is hinged so the mining shovel can drop its load.

MINING SHOVEL

Not all mines are hidden deep beneath the ground. Sometimes, minerals lie close to or on the surface. To get at these minerals,

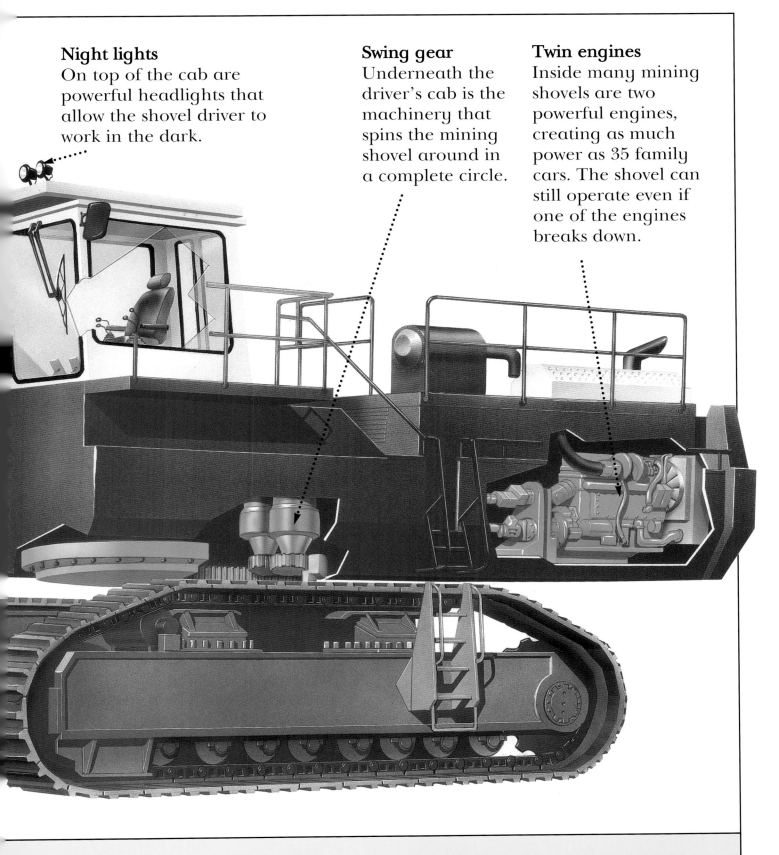

Night lights
On top of the cab are powerful headlights that allow the shovel driver to work in the dark.

Swing gear
Underneath the driver's cab is the machinery that spins the mining shovel around in a complete circle.

Twin engines
Inside many mining shovels are two powerful engines, creating as much power as 35 family cars. The shovel can still operate even if one of the engines breaks down.

huge machines (*see* pages 22-23) dig up the rock, creating enormous mines called opencast mines. One of these machines is a mining shovel. When it has filled its bucket, the driver can spin the shovel around and drop the load into a waiting truck.

Long tunnel

The world's longest rail tunnel is the Seikan rail tunnel in Japan. It is 33.5 miles (54 km) long. It runs under the sea between the main island of Honshu and the island of Hokkaido. Here (*right*) you can see some of the machines used to dig the tunnel.

Under the sea

The Channel Tunnel runs between England and France. Tunnel-boring machines (*see* pages 28-29) took over four years to dig the tunnel. This picture (*left*) shows the exciting moment when the two halves of the tunnel were linked.

tunnel underground.

Cutting coal

In an early underground coal mine, people had to dig the coal out with picks and shovels. Today, machines are used to cut coal from the coal face — the exposed coal on the walls of the mine (*above*).

Exploding walls

This machine (*left*) is used to drill lots of little holes into a mine wall or coal face. The holes are loaded with explosives that are then set off. The wall shatters and falls to the floor. The rubble is gathered and removed.

Cutting head

The cutting head is fitted with 100 cutting rollers and 200 picking teeth. These are made from a very tough metal called tungsten.

Conveyor belt

This belt carries the rubble away from the tunnel face to waiting trucks.

Drive motor

This huge electric motor spins the cutting head. The cutting head rotates about 1.5 to 3 times each minute.

Push and pull

This motor makes sure that the cutting head is in the right position to cut the rock efficiently.

TUNNEL-BORING MACHINE

Creeping forward at a speed of 5 inches (12 cm) a minute, these long machines are

Fixing the segments
The segments lock together snugly and the joints are filled. In some cases, the tunnel may need to be watertight, so segments are bolted together and rubber seals used.

Concrete and iron segments
The tunnel is lined with concrete and iron segments, each weighing up to eight tons!

Carrying the segments
Each segment is lifted from its train car by a special crane. This crane then lifts the segments onto a special trolley that carries them along the tunnel.

used to dig tunnels. These tunnels can run under the seabed, through a mountain, or beneath busy city streets. At the front of a tunnel-boring machine (TBM), there is a huge cutting head that can rotate at different speeds to cut away the rock.

Fantastic facts

- The largest mining excavator ever built is a dragline excavator called Big Muskie. It weighs 12,000 tons and has a bucket capacity of 37,000 gallons (168,000 liters)!

- The Italian inventor and artist Leonardo da Vinci designed the first rotating crane in 1480.

- The pneumatic drill was invented in 1861 by the French engineer Germain Sommeiller. It was first used to build the Mont Cenis Tunnel which runs under the Alps.

- The tallest mobile crane in the world is the Rosenkranz K10001. It weighs nearly 900 tons, but it can lift nearly 1,120 tons. Its arm can reach a height of 663 feet (202 m).

- Caterpillar tracks were invented in 1904 by American inventor Benjamin Holt. They were first used on a tractor in 1908.

- The tunnel-boring machines used to dig the Channel Tunnel were 49 feet (15 m) long and weighed 1,300 tons. Behind them were trains, each some 590 feet (180 m) long and with over 1,000 tons of equipment.

Building words

Backhoe

The extendable hydraulic arm at the rear of a backhoe loader. It digs by using an inward movement.

Caterpillar tracks

These are wide belts that are fixed to a vehicle instead of wheels. They spread the weight of the vehicle over a large area and stop it from sinking into soft ground.

Hydraulic

This refers to objects that are moved or powered by a liquid, such as water or oil. Hydraulic rams are used to move the arms in most diggers.

Internal combustion engine

An engine where the burning of air and fuel occurs inside the engine's cylinders. Steam engines are not internal combustion engines because their fuel is burned outside the engine.

Piston

A rod that fits inside a cylinder and is moved up and down by the pressure of a gas or a liquid.

Pneumatic

This refers to objects that are moved or powered by compressed air, such as a pneumatic drill.

Index

PHOTO CREDITS

Abbreviations: t-top, m-middle, b-bottom, r-right, l-left, c-center.
Pages 5, 9, & 19m — Charles de Vere. 6 & 18t — Roger Vlitos.
6-7, 11m, 12t, & 13 all — Liebherr UK Ltd. 7m — JCB. 7b,
11b, & 18b — Courtesy Finning UK Ltd. 10 all, 12b, 16,
19b, 23b, 26, 26-27, & 28 — Frank Spooner Pictures. 14
both & 15 — Mary Evans Picture Library. 21 — Blaw
Knox. 23t & 27t — Eye Ubiquitous. 24 — Eric
Blackadder. 27b — National Coal Board.

FARM MACHINES

INTRODUCTION

Farming machines have been around for a very long time, helping farmers to grow crops and raise animals. Over the years, these machines have changed greatly, becoming faster and much more powerful. Today, there is a huge number of different machines down on the farm. These help with many jobs, from plowing to harvesting and making food for animals.

STANDARD TRACTOR

Around the farm, the farmer needs a machine that can perform many different roles, from pulling trailers to clearing out milking sheds. The machine that fits this job is the tractor. It can lift and drag heavy objects around the farmyard, and is also tough enough to drive across rugged countryside in all weather conditions. At the same time, the driver's cab is fitted with a tough roll cage. This protects the driver from being crushed if the tractor should tip over.

Many gears

Tractors have to deal with different surfaces, including dry farmyards and muddy fields. To handle these, tractors have many gears to transmit the power from the engine to the driveshaft and the wheels. Some tractors have eighteen forward gears and six reverse gears!

Front wheels

The front wheels of this tractor are much smaller than its rear wheels. These small front wheels are not driven by the engine.

Chunky wheels

The big rear wheels with their chunky tread help the tractor to drive over uneven ground. They also spread the tractor's weight over a larger area. This stops it from squashing the soil, which could harm a growing crop.

Cushion comfort
Some cabs are fitted with seats that are supported on air-filled cushions. These cushions absorb knocks and jolts, giving the farmer a comfortable ride.

Attachment points
Farm machines, such as plows and seed drills, are attached to special points on the tractor. The hydraulic linkage can be raised and lowered to hold the machine at the correct height. The power takeoff (PTO) transfers power from the tractor to the machine.

Tractors are used for

Towing a trailer

The simplest job a tractor can do is to tow something — even the smallest tractors are used to pull trailers (*left*). These trailers can contain anything from harvested crops to manure!

Going up

The front of this tractor (*far right*) has been fitted with two powerful hydraulic arms to lift heavy objects. In this case, they are being used to lift and stack round bales of hay (*see pages 22-23*). The other tractor is linked up to a trailer and is waiting to tow the hay bales away.

lots of different jobs.

In the dark

Some jobs on the farm may need to be done at any time — even in the middle of the night! To work in the dark, tractors are fitted with headlights (*right*).

Leaf blowing

Tractors are not only used on farms. This tractor (*below*) is being used on a golf course. It is towing a machine that blows leaves into a pile so that they can be collected later.

Farm machines have

Animal power

Before steam engines were invented, farm machines, such as plows, were pulled by animals, including horses and cows (*left*). Animals are still used on farms in many parts of the world today!

Engine power

Although not as powerful as today's tractors, the first gasoline-powered tractors (*below right*) changed farming a great deal. They were faster and more powerful than animals, and allowed farmers to work a lot more quickly. The first tractors to use gasoline engines were introduced in the 1890s.

changed over time.

All-purpose machine

In the late 1930s, the engineer Harry Ferguson invented the hydraulic linkage that joined farm machinery to the tractor. It lets the farmer move and use machinery from the tractor's seat. The basic design for this is still used today (*see* pages 4-5).

Steam threshing

Some of the earliest farm engines were powered by steam. Here (*above*), a steam traction engine is powering a threshing machine to separate the grain from the straw.

Cleaner engines

Today's tractor engines need to work very efficiently to help the farmer save money. Efficient engines also give off lower levels of harmful exhaust gases, helping to keep the environment cleaner.

Front attachments

This tractor also has attachment points on its front. This means that a farmer can power and control more than one machine at the same time.

Computer control

Inside the driver's cab is a computer that tells the farmer how the tractor is performing. Because the tractor's wheels might slip in the muddy conditions, the tractor also uses a radar system that can work out the tractor's actual speed!

Rear strength

The back of this tractor can lift a load of over three tons — about the weight of a fully grown elephant!

FOUR-WHEEL-DRIVE TRACTOR

Some of the most powerful farm tractors have four-wheel drive. This means that all four wheels are powered by the engine, instead of just the back two wheels, as in the standard tractor (*see* pages 4-5). Four-wheel drive allows the tractor to find its way over the muddiest terrain. This four-wheel-drive tractor also has a special suspension system that allows it to drive on roads at speeds of up to 50 mph (80 km/h) — nearly twice as fast as other tractors!

Special suspension

The rear wheels on most tractors are linked by a solid rear axle that has little or no suspension. This means that they cannot absorb bumps in the ground very well. All four wheels on this tractor, however, have independent suspension. This reduces the vibration, allowing it to drive faster on all surfaces.

11

Some farms need

Tremendous tractors

This tractor (*below*) needs to be powerful to handle a huge farm. The largest tractor engines can generate 525 horsepower — almost as much as a Formula One racing car!

massive tractors.

Monster machines

The largest tractors in the world, such as this one in Canada (*right*), can weigh nearly 22 tons — that's as much as 340 adults!

Double wheels

To stop the heaviest tractors from squashing and damaging the soil, many of them are fitted with double wheels (*below*). These spread the tractor's weight over a greater area.

Machines are used to

Plowing

Before the farmer can plant a crop, the ground must be prepared. The metal blades of a plow or cultivator are pulled through the ground by a tractor (*right*). These blades break up the soil, making it easier for the farmer to prepare the earth.

Rolling

To prepare the soil even further, a farmer uses a roller (*below left*). Rollers are made up of a number of wide metal rings that are pulled behind a tractor. As the roller moves over the ground, these rings break up any clumps of earth, push any stones into the ground, and squash the soil down to create a good surface for planting.

prepare the ground.

Cultivator

As well as plowing a field, a farmer can use a cultivator (*left*). Cultivators have a number of prongs or blades that are moved through the soil to break it up even more. By breaking up the soil before the crops are planted, cultivators allow more air and water to seep into the earth. This helps the crops to grow.

Seed drill

The farmer plants the crop using a seed drill (*right*). The seeds are held in a large container. As the seed drill is pulled along, the seeds are fed through pipes and dropped into small channels that are cut in the earth by small prongs in front of the pipes. The seeds and the channels are then covered with soil by more small prongs at the rear of the seed drill.

Satellite navigation

Some of the most modern harvesters are fitted with a link to satellites orbiting the earth. These satellites tell the farmer exactly where the harvester is positioned. From this the farmer can work out how much land he or she has harvested.

Cutting

The large reel at the front feeds the crop onto a moving, serrated blade. After the crop is cut, an auger feeds it onto the crop elevator which carries it into the harvester for threshing.

COMBINE HARVESTER

When it comes to harvesting a crop, farmers today have machines that can do the same job that used to take hundreds of

Emptying the load
When the grain tank is full, it is emptied into trucks through this long unloader spout.

Threshing
Inside the harvester is the threshing drum. This has tough metal bars that spin around to beat the crop and separate the grain from the straw and chaff.

Separating the crop
After the threshing drum, the crop passes onto the straw walkers. As the crop moves along these, the grain falls through sieves and is taken to the grain tank at the top of the harvester. The straw passes up and out of the back of the harvester and the lightweight chaff is blown off the grain using a fan.

farm laborers. Combine harvesters can cut the crop and sort the grain out from the straw and waste matter, or chaff.

Some of the largest combine harvesters can cut a strip that is 23 feet (7 m) wide — as much as four adults lying head to toe.

Cutting corn

Some combine harvesters can be fitted with different types of cutting tools to cut different crops, such as sunflowers. Here (*right*), one is harvesting a crop of corn.

Buried treasure

Many crops grow underground, including sugar beet and potatoes They need special harvesters to collect them. This machine (*below*) is harvesting sugar beet. It cuts off the green parts of the plants that grow above ground, and then digs the roots out from the earth.

types of harvester.

Picking grapes

Grapes grow on vines. These are climbing plants that farmers set out in rows. A grape harvester (*right*) is a special machine that drives along between the vines, rubbing the grapes off so that they can be used to make wine.

In a paddy

This small harvester (*left*) is used to harvest rice. It has to drive through the flooded rice fields, called paddies. The harvester has to be small and light to stop it from sinking into the paddies.

Expanding basket
The roof of the basket in which the cotton bolls are collected rises in stages so the picker can hold more cotton.

Engine power
This cotton picker is fitted with a powerful engine. This engine powers the pickers at the front of the machine and helps to squash the cotton bolls after they've been picked.

COTTON PICKER

Cotton plants produce balls of fluffy cotton, called cotton bolls. These are spun out into thread that can be woven

Blowing cotton
Powerful fans at the front blow the picked cotton up through chutes and into the basket.

Automatic steering
This cotton picker is fitted with a special guidance system that steers the machine automatically. This lets the operator concentrate on picking the cotton rather than on keeping the picker on course.

Spinning spikes
The pickers at the front of the machine are made up of spiked drums. As these drums spin, the spikes tear the bolls of cotton away from the plant.

Up and down
There are special sensors at the front of the cotton picker that can detect changes in ground height. The pickers can then move up and down automatically so they stay at the correct height. This ensures that they pick as much of the crop as possible.

to make clothes, carpets, and blankets. Huge machines called cotton pickers are used to harvest the cotton bolls.

These enormous pickers strip the cotton bolls off the plant and collect them in a huge basket at the back.

Tractor power
The baler is pulled by a tractor. The tractor also supplies the power that makes the baler work.

Collecting straw
At the front of the baler is a pronged drum. As this drum rotates, it picks up the hay or straw from the ground and feeds it into the baler.

Back passage
Once the bale is big enough, the machine wraps it in twine. Then the rear of the baler is opened and the bale rolls down a ramp and out of the machine.

BALER

After a crop has been harvested, the field is left covered with the stems of the cut plants. This is called straw, which is used as

Rollers

As hay or straw is fed into the bale chamber, steel rollers around the wall of the chamber roll the hay or straw into a large, round bale.

Round bale

Round bales are better at shedding water than square bales. A large, round hay bale can weigh as much as 1,100 lbs (500 kg) — that's as much as seven adults!

bedding for animals. Hay is dried grass, which can be used to feed animals. Once the hay or straw has dried properly, the farmer uses a baler to collect it into parcels called bales. These bales are either round or square.

23

Machines are used to

Green crops

Farmers make fodder, which is used to feed animals, from green or unripe crops. These green crops can include grass or unripe corn. Here (*right*), unripe corn is being cut and pulped along with its stalks.

Cutting grass

Here (*left*), a tractor is powering a cutter to chop down grass. As the cutter moves forward, huge blades spin around, cutting the grass. This cut grass is then funneled into rows, called swaths, that make it easier to collect. However, before the grass is collected to make fodder, the farmer leaves the swaths out for a day or two so the grass wilts a little. These swaths are then collected using a forage harvester (*see right*).

Collecting the grass

As the forage harvester moves forward, the spiked drum at the front picks up the swath and feeds it into the machine (*above*). Here, the grass is chopped up finely before it is fed into a waiting trailer and carried off for storage.

Silage clamp

The green crops have to be stored before they turn into silage. They can be stored in large towers called silos, open yards called silage clamps (*left*), or pits. They can also be collected into bales and wrapped in plastic.

Huge engines

The engines used in tractor pulling competitions need to be big. Some of the biggest produce a massive 7,000 horsepower — that's more than 11 times the power produced by a Formula One racing car!

Driver

Like all other motor sports, the driver must wear a crash helmet and dress from head to toe in flameproof clothing

Little and large

The huge rear wheels give the tractor as much grip as possible. The front wheels are tiny in comparison. They are only used to steer the tractor. Sometimes, they can be lifted clear off the ground.

TRACTOR PULLING

Tractor pulling developed from competitions between farmers to see who had the strongest tractor. Today, it has

Movable weight

During the pull, the weight moves along the sled, toward the tractor. This has the effect of increasing the weight on the drag plate, making it harder for the tractor to pull the sled along.

Control cab

At the rear of the sled sits a referee. He or she sets the speed at which the weight moves forward, making it harder or easier for the tractor to pull the sled. There is also a switch that can turn off the tractor's power in case of an emergency.

Drag plate

At the front of the sled is the drag plate. As the tractor pulls the sled along, this plate is pushed into the ground until it creates so much friction that the tractor is forced to stop.

become the most powerful motor sport in the world. Tractor drivers compete to see whose tractor can pull a heavy sled the farthest. Their specially built tractors are fitted with massive engines and enormous rear wheels.

Farm machines come

Tractor on stilts

This tractor (*above*) is raised on specially built axles and suspension. This enables it to raise both itself and spraying equipment above the crop so the chemicals can be sprayed properly.

Long arm

Sometimes farmers need to pile objects high. To do this, they can use a telescopic handler, which has a long, extendable arm (*left*).

n all shapes and sizes.

Tracked tractor

This tractor (*below*) is fitted with caterpillar tracks. These tracks reduce the pressure on the ground and therefore reduce the damage the tractor may cause to soil.

Digging drains

The massive claw on the front of this bulldozer (*right*) is sunk into the ground and dragged backward to dig drainage channels. These drainage channels allow water to drain away from a field so the field won't get waterlogged, which damages crops.

Fantastic facts

- There are millions and millions of tractors in the world today.

- The first successful mechanical seed drill was invented in 1701 by a farmer called Jethro Tull.

- The invention of the cotton gin by American Eli Whitney in 1793 allowed farmers to grow cotton on a large scale for the first time.

- In 1834 an American farmer called Cyrus Hall McCormick invented the first successful harvesting machine.

- In 1837 an American blacksmith called John Deere invented the first steel plow. Earlier iron plows got caked in mud, but mud slipped off the new steel plow blades, creating a cleaner furrow in which seeds could be planted.

- Two American brothers, John and Hiram Pitts, invented a threshing machine in 1838.

- John Froehlich, a blacksmith from Iowa, built the first successful gasoline-powered farm vehicle in 1892.

Farming words

Bale

A bundle of hay or straw. Rectangular bales can weigh up to 2,200 lbs (1,000 kg)!

Caterpillar tracks

These are wide belts that are fixed to a vehicle instead of wheels. They spread the weight of the vehicle over a large area and stop it from damaging the soil too much.

Fodder

Green crops, such as grass or unripe corn, which have been stored for a time in a silo, pit, or open yard. After it has fermented, fodder is used to feed farm animals.

Four-wheel drive

This is when all four wheels on a vehicle are powered by the engine. Four-wheel-drive vehicles can pull a heavier load over rougher ground than two-wheel-drive vehicles.

Suspension

A system of springs and other devices that makes the ride of a vehicle smoother.

Threshing drum

A barred barrel found inside a combine harvester. As this barrel spins, the bars separate a crop into the grain and the unwanted straw.

Index

PHOTO CREDITS
Abbreviations: t-top, m-middle, b-bottom, r-right, l-left, c-center.
Pages 4, 6-7, 18t, 22, & 28t — Massey Ferguson Tractors.
6, 7t, 13b, & 14 — Renault Agriculture. 7b, 19t, & 29b —
Charles de Vere. 8 both, 9, 13t — Mike Williams/Media
Mechanics. 11, 15t, & 25b — JCB Landpower Ltd. 12-13, 14b,
15m, 18b, 24b, 25t, & 29m — Peter Hill/Media Mechanics. 16 &
28b — Claas UK. 19b — Spectrum Colour Library. 20 — John
Deere. 24t — USDA. 26 — Frank Spooner Pictures.

LOOK INSIDE MACHINES

RACING CARS

JON RICHARDS

Franklin Watts
London • Sydney

CONTENTS

INTRODUCTION

Motor racing is very exciting. Cars zoom around racetracks at high speeds, trying to finish the course in the shortest possible time. There are many different types of racing cars in different parts of the world. They can be simple and small, like go-karts, or powerful and packed full of high-tech equipment, like Formula One racing cars.

Fuel tank
Fuel for the race is pumped into the tank behind the driver.

Cockpit
The drivers sit in very small cockpits. From here they control the speed of the car and steer it in the right direction.

Exhaust
This metal pipe carries waste gases away from the engine and out behind the car.

OLD RACER

This car raced in Grand Prix during the late 1950s. Even then, racing cars looked very different from normal road cars.

4

Engine
The engine for this old racing car sits in front of the driver. Today, the engine in a Formula One car is behind the driver.

Wheels
Unlike modern racing wheels, these wheels have wire spokes. They are also much thinner than modern racing wheels.

Radiator
The radiator helps to stop the engine from overheating.

They had much more powerful engines, specially built bodies to help them go faster, and their drivers sat in small cockpits.

However, these old front-engined cars were replaced by cars with their engines placed behind the driver.

Racing has changed

Modern racing cars

This 1970s Formula One car (*right*) is very similar to today's racing vehicles. Its engine is behind the driver, it has fat tires to help it grip the track, and it has large "wings" to help the car drive faster (*see* page 8).

Cockpit

Rear wing

Rear wheel

Changing shapes

Over the years, designers and mechanics have looked at ways of making the cars move through the air more easily. As a result, today's cars are more streamlined than the bulkier shapes of the earliest racers (*left*).

a lot over the years.

Strange racing cars

People who build racing cars have tried many ways to make their cars go faster. These have included making the engines very powerful and even building a car that had six wheels (*right*).

Six-wheeled racing car

Nose

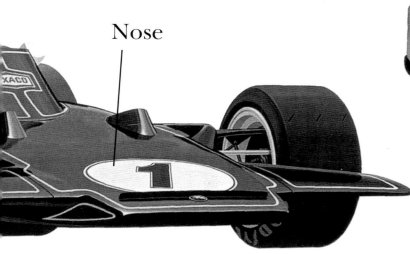

Running start

Some races used to begin with the drivers running to their cars across the track (*right*). However, this has now been stopped because it became dangerous for the drivers.

Wings

As air flows over these "wings," it pushes the car down onto the track. This helps the tires to grip, stopping them from slipping. This allows the car to go faster (*see* page 19).

Roll bar

The roll bar is found just behind the driver's head. It protects the driver if the car turns over.

Cockpit

The driver sits in a cockpit made from a tough material called carbon fiber. This protects the driver in a crash.

INDY CAR

This type of racer is called an Indy car. It has a specially designed body, with fins and wings, and a very powerful engine. These mean that the Indy car can zoom around tracks at speeds of over 200 mph (320 km/h) — that's more than twice as fast as a normal road car!

Indy cars are often raced around oval-shaped tracks. The oval tracks have banked corners that are raised on the outside. These let the cars go even faster!

Tires
An Indy car can use two types of tires. One is fitted in dry weather. It is called a "slick." The other type is fitted in wet weather. It has a deep pattern on its surface to help the car drive in the rain.

Tire walls

Some parts of a racetrack are lined with walls made from stacks of old tires (*above*). These provide a springy barrier to stop cars if they crash into them.

Gravel traps

Around other parts of a racetrack there may be large areas covered with gravel. When a car comes off the track, the gravel slows the car down, gradually and safely (*above*).

to keep a race safe.

Tough on the track

Because racing cars are traveling very quickly, any crashes that occur can be dangerous (*above*). To protect the drivers, parts of the cars are made from very strong materials, such as carbon fiber (*see* page 8).

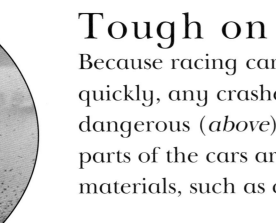

The pace car

After a bad crash, a pace car is sent onto the track. The racing cars have to slow down and line up behind the pace car (*right*) until the wreckage has been cleared.

Engine
This must be very powerful to drive the car quickly. It must also run for a very long time without developing any faults.

Driving seat
The driver is held securely in place by a specially shaped seat and a strong harness.

Brakes
During a race, the brakes of a racing car get very hot as they are used to slow the car — sometimes they can glow with the heat!

ENDURANCE RACER
Many races can go on for a very long time — some of them can last for 24 hours! They are called endurance races.

Windshield
The windshield of an endurance racer is very large. This gives the driver as clear a view of the road as possible.

Wing mirrors
These special mirrors on the side of the car help the drivers to see behind them.

Headlights
During a 24-hour race the cars have to drive through the night. To help the drivers see, the cars have bright headlights.

During these races, teams of two or three drivers take turns to drive the car as far as possible within the time limit.

When the car pulls into the pits (*see* pages 20-21) one driver leaps out of the car and another gets in to continue the race.

Race teams have lots

A race team

The drivers are only a small part of the entire race team (*right*). Behind them are the team managers, engineers, mechanics, and technicians who work on the cars at each race. Then, at the team headquarters, there are designers and builders. They work on the racing car's design and try to improve its performance.

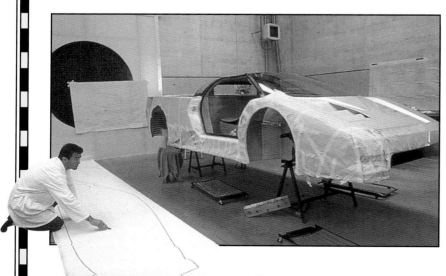

New designs

Designers and builders use the latest technology to create faster cars (*left*). They can see how these new models will perform by testing them using wind tunnels and computers.

# of people in them.

Team trucks

Massive trucks (*above*) are used to carry the team's equipment. Inside them is everything the team needs, including the cars, spare tires, and even spare engines.

Mechanics

A number of mechanics travel with the team's cars. They fit engines into each of the cars and adjust other parts of the cars to suit the conditions for each race (*right*).

What it takes to

Helmet

Helmets

To protect their heads, drivers wear helmets made from a tough material called fiber glass. The helmets have a tube through which the drivers can drink. There is also a radio to keep them in touch with the pits.

Driving suit

Gloves

Body protection

The driving suit, gloves, and boots are made from fireproof materials. Beneath these may be another layer of fireproof underclothes, including a balaclava that covers the head and face.

Boots

be a racing driver.

Training

Driving a racing car during a long race is very tiring. To stay fit drivers have to watch what they eat and get regular exercise (*right*).

In the cockpit

In some racing cars the drivers have to squeeze into a tight cockpit where there is little room to move (*left*). In front of them are the instruments and the steering wheel.

Examining figures

The car is fitted with sensors that record what the drivers do. These figures are sent back to the pits by radio. The drivers and mechanics can then look at these figures to see how the car can be driven faster (*right*).

Engine
The powerful engine in this racing car is in front of the driver.

RALLY CAR

Not all racing cars are driven on roads. Rally cars race each other over almost any kind of ground, from dirt tracks to snow, and even through large deserts! These cars have to be specially altered so that they can cope with very rough ground.

Inside the rally car, a codriver sits next to the driver. He tells the driver what corners or obstacles are coming next along the track. The driver can then set the speed and direction of the car to match the course.

Spoiler

The rear wing, or spoiler, acts like the wing of an Indy car (*see* page 8). The mechanics have to set the spoiler carefully. If the air flowing over the spoiler pushes down too much it would slow the car down.

Safety cage

This is a special cage made out of tough metal bars. It protects the driver and codriver if the car crashes.

Suspension

Springs and pistons absorb the bumps as the car drives over rough ground. They also stop the car from rocking around too much.

Sometimes a car has

The pits

Cars may pull into the pits during a race. These are places where the mechanics can work on the car (*right*). They may need to change tires, add more fuel, swap drivers, or replace a broken part.

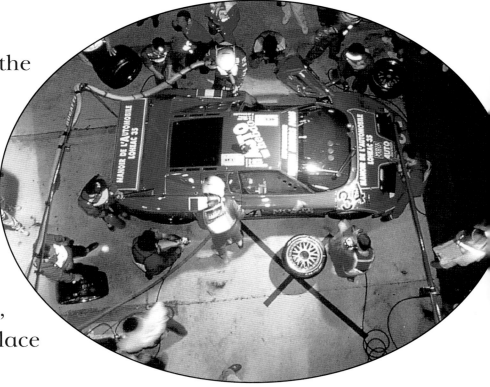

Fill the tank

Racing cars use up a lot of fuel. When they come into the pits, an exact amount of fuel is pumped into the fuel tank (*left*). This fuel lets the car finish the next part of the race.

to pull into the pits.

Pit safety

Because there is a lot of fuel around the pits, accidents can sometimes occur (*above*). Mechanics have to wear fireproof suits just like the drivers (*see* page 16).

Nighttime pits

During endurance races, mechanics in the pits need to be alert throughout the whole event. A pit stop could occur at any time — even in the middle of the night (*right*)!

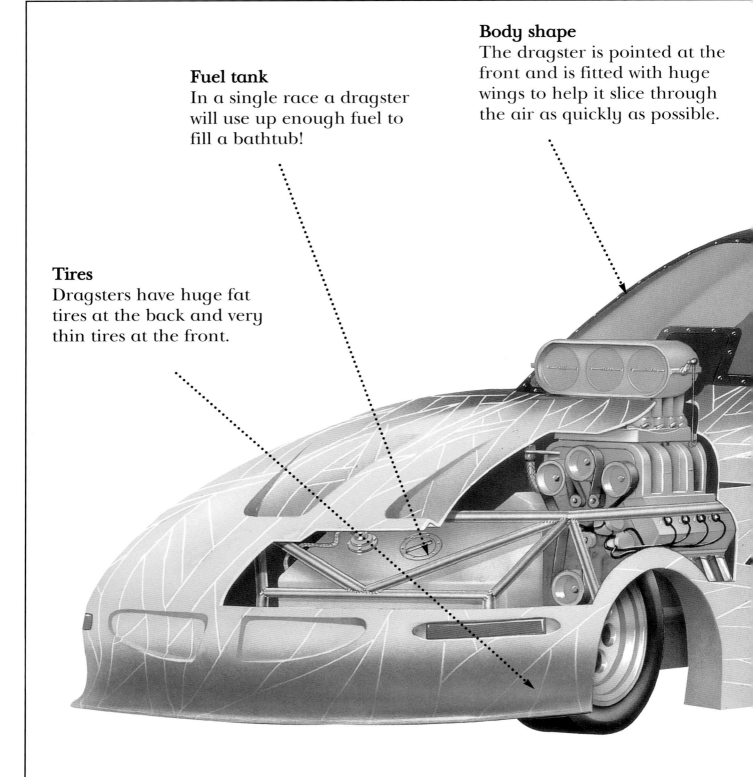

Fuel tank
In a single race a dragster will use up enough fuel to fill a bathtub!

Body shape
The dragster is pointed at the front and is fitted with huge wings to help it slice through the air as quickly as possible.

Tires
Dragsters have huge fat tires at the back and very thin tires at the front.

DRAGSTER

Dragsters are specially built cars that are designed for one thing — racing as quickly as possible along a straight track.

Cockpit

Inside the dragster is a safety cage similar to one in a rally car (*see* page 19). The cockpit is also fitted with a fire extinguisher.

Parachute

At the back of a dragster is a parachute. At the end of a race the driver releases this to help slow the car down.

Wheelie bar

This special bar at the back stops the dragster from flipping over when it zooms off.

Before they start, the drivers will spin their wheels. This "burning rubber" helps the tires to grip. When the signal is given, they whiz off down the track to see who can cross the finish line in the quickest time. Races can last as little as five seconds!

Many events happen

On the grid

A qualifying session is held before a race. During this session, drivers race to decide their position on the starting lineup, called the grid (*left*). The fastest driver starts at the front of the grid, called pole position.

Overtaking

During the race, cars compete to take the lead. To do this a driver must overtake (*below*) all the other cars. Getting to the front requires a lot of skill.

during the race.

The finish

The winner of the race is the first past the finish line when all the laps have been driven. When the winner crosses the line a race official waves a black-and-white checkered flag (*right*).

On the podium

The winner of the race goes onto the podium, as well as the drivers who finish second and third. Here they receive their trophies and sometimes spray fountains of champagne over each other (*left*).

Spoiler
Mechanics adjust the stock car's spoiler (*see* page 19) before each race to give the best performance.

The cockpit
In front of the driver are the dials and switches that help the driver control the car and show how the car is performing.

Cockpit safety
The cockpit is surrounded by a strong safety cage made of metal bars. It is also fitted with a firefighting system.

STOCK CAR

These powerful machines are road cars that have been converted into racing cars. Most of the time they race around oval

Paintwork
The bodies of many racing cars are covered in brightly colored logos. These are the sponsors' symbols. The sponsors give money to the racing team.

The engine
Beneath the hood is a very powerful engine. It is nearly ten times as powerful as the engine in a small family car!

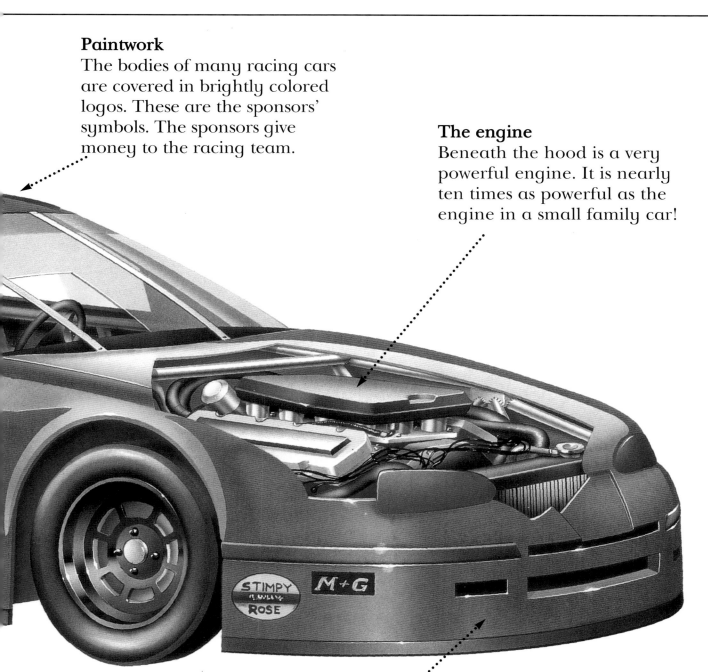

STIMPY IS COOL ROSE

M+G

Skirting
The front of the car is fitted with an extra piece of body kit, called a skirt. This skirt stops air from flowing under the car. If air did get under the car it would slow the car down.

courses like Indy cars (*see* pages 8-9). The cars may be bunched together at very high speed for the whole race. The slightest nudge can result in a spectacular crash! Because of this each car is built to protect the driver from any serious harm.

There are lots of

Hot rods

Put a powerful engine in an old car, paint it brightly, and you have a Hot Rod (*above*). Like dragsters, these cars are raced against each other on a straight track.

Dune buggies

In desert countries, lightweight cars called buggies race each other over sand dunes (*below*). These cars are little more than a safety cage and an engine on four wheels!

other racing cars.

Old timers

Very old cars (some nearly 100 years old) are still raced in many parts of the world (*right*). With these cars it is not so much winning the race as completing the course in one piece!

Go-karts

Although these racing cars are very small, they can still drive very quickly (*left*). Many of today's top racing drivers began their careers by racing go-karts.

Fantastic facts

• The first Grand Prix race was held at Le Mans in France in 1906. It was won by the French driver, Ferenc Szisz.

• The world's longest rally ever held covered a distance of 19,329 miles (31,107 km) from London, England, to Sydney, Australia. It took place between August and September 1977.

• The fastest speed achieved by a dragster over a 440-yard (400-meter) track is 316 mph (506 km/h). This was achieved in Topeka, Kansas.

• German Michael Schumacher has broken many Formula One records. He has won the drivers' championship seven times. He also holds the record for races won and, as of 2006, for pole positions.

Racing words

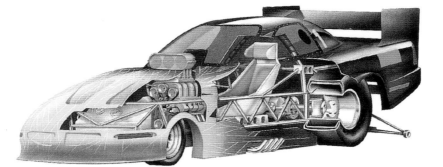

Cockpit
The part of a racing car where the driver sits. It contains the car's controls and the instruments that show how the car is performing.

Exhaust
A pipe, or number of pipes, that carry waste gases away from the engine.

Grid
The lineup of racing cars at the start of a race.

Pit area
The part of a racetrack where mechanics can work on a racing car during a race.

Safety cage
A cage of strong metal bars inside the racing car. This protects the driver in the event of a crash.

Skirting
The piece of body kit that runs around the base of a car.

Slick tire
A tire with no tread that is used in dry weather conditions.

Suspension
Systems of springs and pistons that absorb bumps on the road and stop the car from rocking around too much.

Index

PHOTO CREDITS
Abbreviations: t-top, m-middle, b-bottom, r-right, l-left, c-center

Pages 4 & 7 – Hulton Getty Collection. 9, 10b, 12, 14b, 17t & b, 20t, 21b, 24 both, 25, 26 & 29 – Frank Spooner Pictures. 10t, 11b, 14-15, 15b & 17m – Empics. 11t, 20b, 21t, 24-25 & 28 both – Rex Features. 15t – Renault UK. 18 – Ford UK. 22 – Neil Smith.

LOOK INSIDE MACHINES

JETLINERS

JON RICHARDS

Franklin Watts
London • Sydney

© Aladdin Books Ltd

Designed and
produced by
Aladdin Books Ltd

Editor
Simon Beecroft
Consultant
Colin Uttley
Design
David West
Children's Book Design
Designer
Robert Perry
Illustrators
Simon Tegg & Mike Saunders
Picture Research
Brooks Krikler Research

CONTENTS

INTRODUCTION

The world's first jetliner entered service over fifty years ago. In the short space of time since then, jetliners have improved, and now carry people to all corners of the globe. They also come in all shapes and sizes. These range from tiny business jets that can only carry a few people over a short distance, to huge jumbo jets that can carry hundreds of people to the other side of the world.

Going up and down

These parts of the wing are called ailerons. The pilot could move the ailerons up and down to make the plane bank or turn.

Flight deck

The flight crew sat in the flight deck at the front of the plane. The flight crew of a 707 was made up of the pilot, first officer, and the flight engineer.

Nosewheels

The nosewheels sat under the front of the plane. When the plane was in the air they were tucked up inside the plane's body.

BOEING 707

The first experimental jet-powered plane flew in 1939. However, it was another 15 years before planes powered by jets

Passengers
Some 707s could carry
nearly 190 people, sitting six
across the body of the plane.

Main landing gear
The main landing gear on a
707 had two sets of wheels that
were found beneath each side
of the wing.

Engine
The 707 had four jet
engines, two beneath
each side of the wing.

carried passengers all over the
world. One of the earliest jet
airliners to go into service was
the Boeing 707. It was first used
in 1958 by Pan American
Airways to carry people across
the Atlantic Ocean between
Europe and the United States.

It takes a lot to

Designing

Aircraft designers need to create a plane that meets the needs of an airline and its passengers. The designers can use a computer to help draw what the plane will look like (*left*).

Giant jigsaw

The parts of a jet airliner are built separately and then put together like the pieces of an enormous jigsaw puzzle (*below*).

build a jetliner.

Testing the engine

Jet engines must work for many hours, carrying a plane over very long distances. A lot of checks and tests are carried out to make sure that the jet engines work without developing problems (*right*).

Test flying

Once the plane has been built it must be tested to see how it flies. Pilots will push the plane to its limits to see how well it flies in extreme conditions in the air (*above*).

Air conditioning
This hole collects air for the plane's air conditioning system. This keeps the inside of the aircraft at a constant, comfortable temperature.

Air brake
This special flap at the rear of the plane pops out when the plane comes in to land. It helps to slow the plane down very quickly.

Whisper engines
The special engines on the BAe 146 are very quiet. This means that the plane can fly over towns and cities where noise pollution laws are very strict.

High wing
The wing on this plane is set on top of the body. Compare it with the other planes in the book.

SHORT-HAUL JET
Not all jet airliners need to be very big, or fly very long distances. This jet can only carry about 100 people. It is known as a short-haul jet because it is only used to carry passengers on short flights. It is called the British Aerospace (BAe) 146. Its special design allows it to take off and land using very short runways — a jumbo jet needs a runway more than twice as long as the one used by this jet! This makes it an ideal plane for inner-city airports.

Radar
The radar at the front of the aircraft tells the pilots where they are going, which other planes are in the area, or what the weather is like up ahead.

A jetliner has many

In control

The flight crew sit on the flight deck at the front of the plane (*above*). In front of them are the controls and dials that help them to fly the plane.

The galley

This is where the food and drinks are stored. These are delivered to the passengers using special carts (*left*).

different parts to it.

Sitting comfortably

The passengers sit in rows of seats in the passenger cabin. These seats can have televisions to entertain the passengers (*left*) or they can lean back to let the passengers sleep.

The cargo hold

The large space beneath the passenger cabin is used to store the passengers' luggage during the flight. It can also be filled with freight that is being carried to another country. This is loaded through huge doors in the side of the plane (*right*).

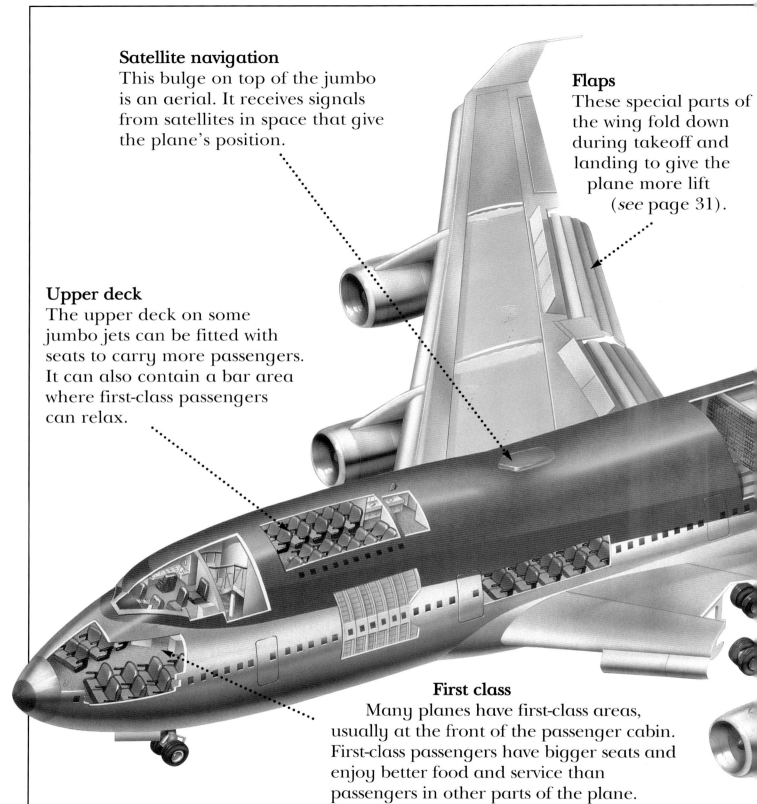

Satellite navigation
This bulge on top of the jumbo is an aerial. It receives signals from satellites in space that give the plane's position.

Flaps
These special parts of the wing fold down during takeoff and landing to give the plane more lift (*see* page 31).

Upper deck
The upper deck on some jumbo jets can be fitted with seats to carry more passengers. It can also contain a bar area where first-class passengers can relax.

First class
Many planes have first-class areas, usually at the front of the passenger cabin. First-class passengers have bigger seats and enjoy better food and service than passengers in other parts of the plane.

JUMBO JET

The Boeing 747 is one of the largest passenger jets in the world. It carries about 525 people, over two decks.

Rudder

This part of the plane's tail can be moved from side to side by the pilot, helping the plane to turn in either direction. ......

Cargo

The rear part of this jumbo jet has been equipped to carry cargo. This can be loaded onto the plane through a massive door in the side of the aircraft.

The bulge at the top of the plane contains the flight deck, where the pilots control the plane, and an extra passenger deck. In 2005, the world's largest passenger plane was unveiled. The Airbus A380 is a twin-decked craft carrying even more people than the jumbo jet.

Airport

Airports can be massive places (*right*). Passengers board their planes at huge buildings called terminals. Once the plane is loaded and all of the passengers are on board, it is ready for takeoff.

Taxiing

The plane leaves the terminal and then moves, or taxis, to an available runway (*left*). The pilot then increases the power of the engines and the plane roars down the runway to take off and begin its flight.

during a jet's flight.

Air-traffic control

When the plane is in the air, air-traffic controllers on the ground (*left*) check its route and tell the pilots where to go. The plane's position is shown on a screen in front of them.

Landing

At the end of a flight, the plane descends and slows down its speed before coming down to land on a runway with its landing gear down (*below*).

The flight crew

Most jetliners are flown by two people, the pilot and the copilot. Some older planes have a third crew member, the flight engineer (*right*). The flight engineer checks that everything on the plane is working correctly.

Flight simulator

Pilots use special machines called flight simulators to learn how to fly and to practice even after they have qualified (*left*). Flight simulators mimic a flight in a plane.— even its movements!

a jetliner in the air.

Engineers

To make sure that the plane is flying safely and smoothly, engineers check its parts between each flight (*above*).

Cabin steward

The cabin stewards look after the passengers during the flight. They make sure that the people are secured in their seats before takeoff and they serve them with food and drinks while the plane is in the air (*right*).

Fuel tanks
The fuel is kept in huge tanks
found in the wing and tailplane.
These tanks can hold enough
fuel to fill nearly 1,500 bathtubs!

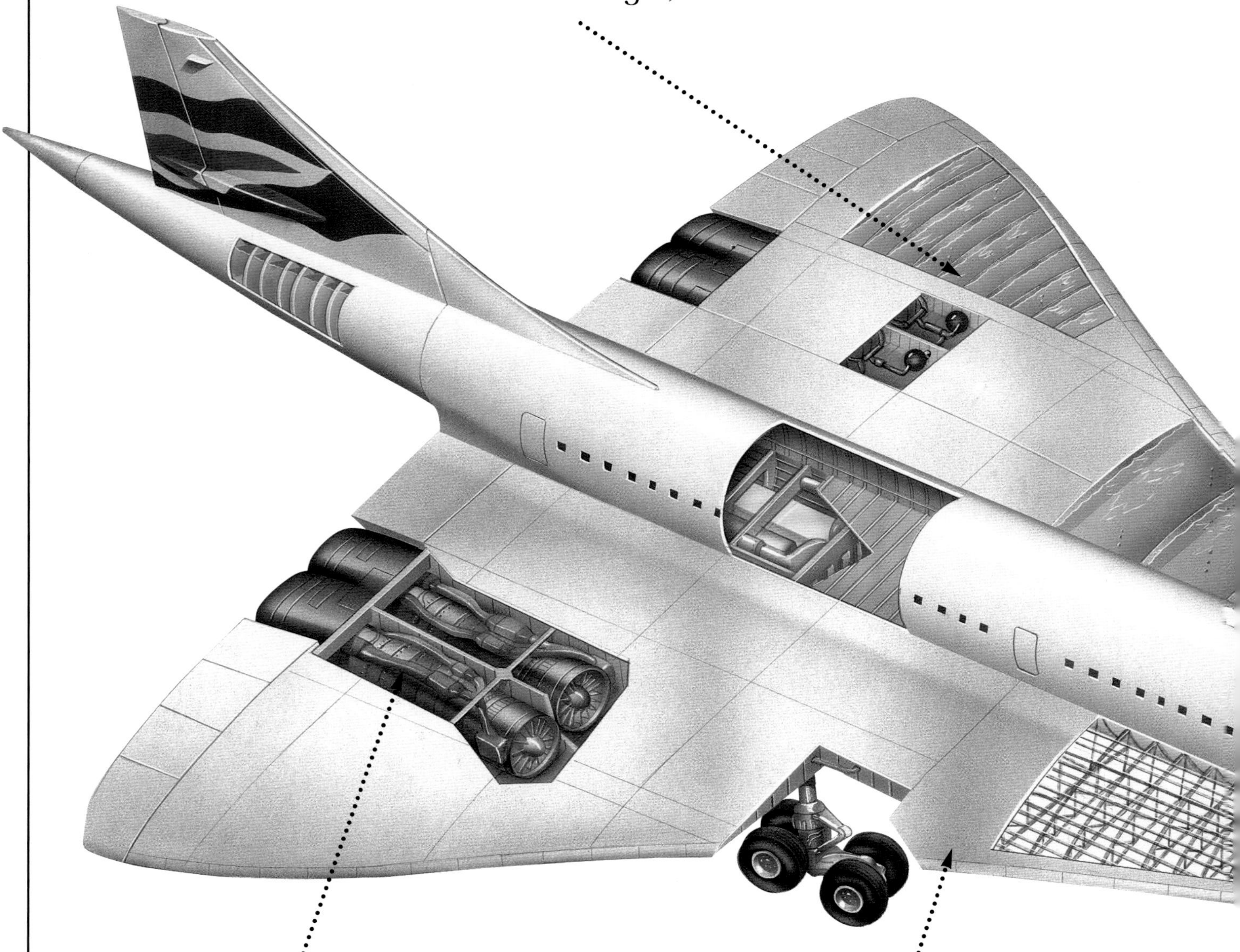

Engines
Concorde has four very powerful
engines. Two are found sitting
just under each side of the wing.

Wing shape
Concorde has a single,
very large triangle-shaped
wing. This is called a delta-
wing design.

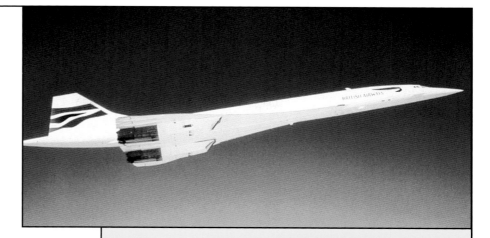

Passenger cabin
The slim body of Concorde means that it can only carry 144 passengers.

CONCORDE

Concorde was the fastest jetliner in the world. It could fly at 1,360 mph (2,180 km/h) — that's twice as fast as the speed of sound. Because of this, Concorde could cross the Atlantic Ocean between Europe and the United States in just three hours! When it travelled faster than the speed of sound, it created a sonic boom. This bang worried many people and meant that Concorde was banned from flying faster than sound over land. Concorde was finally retired from service in 2003.

The nose
Concorde's pointed nose is hinged so that it droops during landing and takeoff. This lets the pilots see the ground.

Preparing a jetliner

Refueling

An airliner uses a lot of fuel during each flight. Before it can take off for the next flight more fuel is pumped into its fuel tanks from gas tankers (*above*).

Luggage

Once the plane has come to a stop, the passengers' luggage is unloaded from the cargo hold (*right*). Once empty, the luggage for the next flight can be loaded on board.

for the next flight.

Safety checks
Before a jetliner can take off, all parts of it must be checked by engineers (*see pages 16-17*). These checks include looking at the plane's undercarriage to see if anything has been damaged or worn (*right*).

Engine damage
Air mechanics will also check the working parts inside a jet engine to see if they have become worn or damaged (*left*).

Luggage
The passengers' luggage is stored in huge cargo holds in the bottom of the jetliner.

Wide body
The body of a Boeing 777 is wide enough to fit ten seats across it.

Folding wings
The wing tips of a few 777s are designed to fold up when the plane is taxiing. This lets it travel along narrow taxiways and gates at some airports.

BOEING 777

The Boeing 777 is one of the most modern jetliners in use today. Using the latest technology and extremely powerful

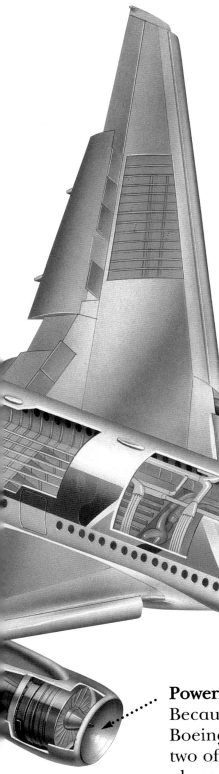

All-seeing
Cameras on the underside of the Boeing 777 let the pilots see the nosewheel and beneath the wing. This is very helpful when the plane is taxiing.

Helpful computers
The Boeing 777 is fitted with the latest equipment. This includes "fly-by-wire" technology, where computers help the pilot to fly the plane.

Powerful engines
Because the engines on the Boeing 777 are so powerful, only two of them are used to fly the plane — a jumbo jet uses four.

engines, this jetliner is far more efficient and a lot less expensive to run than the much older Boeing 747 (*see* pages 12-13).

Inside its extra-wide body, the Boeing 777 can carry nearly as many passengers as a jumbo jet!

Many things make

Firefighters

Airport firefighters (*left*) have to wear special suits when they are tackling a blaze. These suits protect them from the heat of an aircraft fire.

Fire trucks

All airports have fire trucks (*below*) in case of an emergency. These trucks can race quickly to the scene and cover the fire with a thick blanket of foam.

flying very safe.

The black box

Inside every jetliner are some boxes that record the plane's actions. They are called black boxes (*right*). They are built to be tough so that, in the event of an accident, they can be recovered and investigators can find out what went wrong.

Escape slide

If an aircraft is in trouble on the ground, the passengers and crew may need to get out quickly. Special chutes inflate on the sides of the plane (*above*) and the people can slide down them to safety.

TURBOPROP

Even though this plane has propellers, it is still a jetliner. Its two engines are called turboprops. These are a special type of jet engine that turns a propeller (*see* below). The aircraft is called a Jetstream and it is very small indeed. It is used to take small numbers of people over short distances.

Fuel tanks
Like larger jetliners, the Jetstream stores its fuel in fuel tanks that are found in the wing.

Aerial
This aerial on the roof o the Jetstream helps the pilots keep in touch with different airports.

Turboprops
As air flows through the turboprop engine, it turns small fans called turbines. These turbines turn a shaft which turns the propeller at the front of the engine.

Passengers

The passenger compartment can carry about 20 people, or it can be converted into a luxury flying meeting room for business people.

Luggage

A small compartment at the rear of the Jetstream holds all of the passengers' luggage.

Jetliners are used for

Hide and seek

This plane (*below*) has been developed from an old jetliner. It is used by the British Royal Navy to search for enemy ships and submarines. It is also used in air-sea rescue, to find sailors and ships that are lost at sea.

Flight deck

Business jets

Very small jets, such as this one (*left*), can be used to carry business people from meeting to meeting.

a number of jobs.

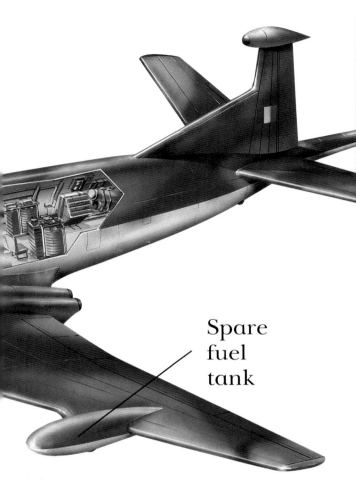

Spare
fuel
tank

Heavy lifting

This Galaxy transport jet
(*above*) is used by the military.
Its huge body contains an
enormous cargo hold. The
plane can carry troops,
equipment, armored vehicles,
and even tanks!

Air Force One

Any plane that the
President of the United
States flies in carries the
call-sign "Air Force
One." Typically, the
President flies in a
specially converted
Boeing 747 (*right*).

Fantastic Facts

• The world's first jetliner was the de Haviland Comet. It first carried passengers in May 1952 on a flight from England to Italy.

• The world's busiest airport is Hartsfield-Jackson Atlanta International in Georgia. In 2005 there were 980,197 takeoffs and landings and an amazing 88.4 million people passed through it.

• Edwards Air Force Base in the United States has the world's longest runway. It stretches for 7.5 miles (11.9 km) in the desert of California.

• In March 1989, a Russian Antonov An-225 lifted a cargo weighing a staggering 172 tons — that's the same as lifting over fifty elephants!

Jet words

Ailerons

These are found on the rear of the wing. The pilot moves them up and down to make the plane bank and turn.

Flight deck

The part of a plane from where the pilot controls the jet.

Fly-by-wire

Some jets may be fitted with fly-by-wire technology. This means that a computer helps the pilot to fly the plane.

Jet engine

An engine that moves a plane forward by creating a jet of fast-moving gases.

Lift

The force created when air flows quickly over a specially shaped wing. This force pushes a plane up into the air.

Rudder

A part of the fin at the rear of the plane. The pilot can move this back and forth to help the plane turn.

Taxiing

The movement of a plane along the ground.

Turboprop

A special type of engine that uses a jet engine to turn a propeller.

Index

PHOTO CREDITS
Abbreviations: t-top, m-middle, b-bottom, r-right, l-left, c-centre.
Pages 4, 9, 10t, 12, 19, 22, 24 both, 25t, & 28 both – Frank Spooner Pictures. 6 both, 7b, & 15b – Airbus Industrie. 7t – Pratt & Whitney. 10b, 11b, 20b, 21 both, & 26 – Aviation Picture Library. 11t – Virgin Air. 14t, 16t, & 27 – Solution Pictures. 14b, 16b, 17t, & 20t – Lufthansa. 15t – Civil Aviation Authority. 17b – Pan Am. 25b – Rex Features.

LOOK INSIDE MACHINES

FIRE
FIGHTERS

JON KIRKWOOD

Franklin Watts
London • Sydney

Designed and produced by
Aladdin Books Ltd

Editor
Jon Richards
Consultant
Steve Allman
Design
David West Children's
Books Design
Designer
Robert Perry
Illustrators
Simon Tegg & Graham White
Picture Research
Brooks Krikler Research

CONTENTS

INTRODUCTION

Fires can be very dangerous. All over the world, men and women are specially trained to fight fires in all kinds of places. These can be far out at sea, up tall buildings, or deep in forests. Fire fighters are also involved in other types of emergency. They often have to rescue people trapped underground and even deal with flooding.

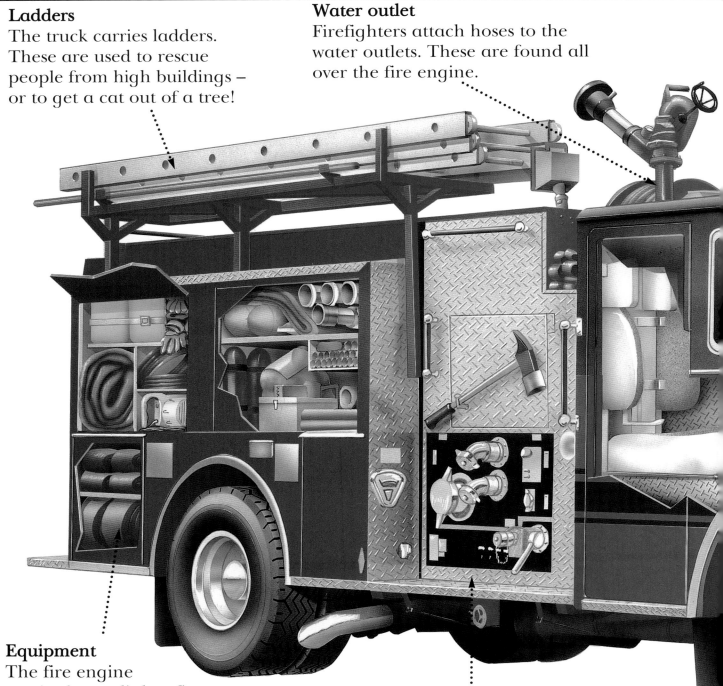

Ladders
The truck carries ladders.
These are used to rescue
people from high buildings –
or to get a cat out of a tree!

Water outlet
Firefighters attach hoses to the
water outlets. These are found all
over the fire engine.

Equipment
The fire engine
carries hoses, lights, first-
aid equipment, breathing
equipment (*see* page 16),
and firefighters' axes.

Control panel
The control panel operates
the pump that pushes water
along the hoses.

FIRE ENGINE

Fire engines race down streets to get to a
blaze. Their lights are flashing and sirens
are blaring to clear a path through traffic.

Siren and lights
The flashing lights and noisy siren warn people that the fire engine is coming.

Cab
The driver sits in the front to steer the truck. The rest of the firefighters sit in the cab behind.

Engine
The engine provides the power to drive the fire truck. It is much more powerful than a car engine.

The truck carries a team of firefighters. It also holds all the equipment they need to cope with many situations. This includes a big tank full of water. This holds enough water to fill over 40 bathtubs! The water is pumped out through the hoses.

Fire trucks come in

Steam engine

Early fire trucks were powered by steam (*left* and *below*). Water was heated in a boiler to produce steam. This gave the truck's pump the power to push water through the hoses.

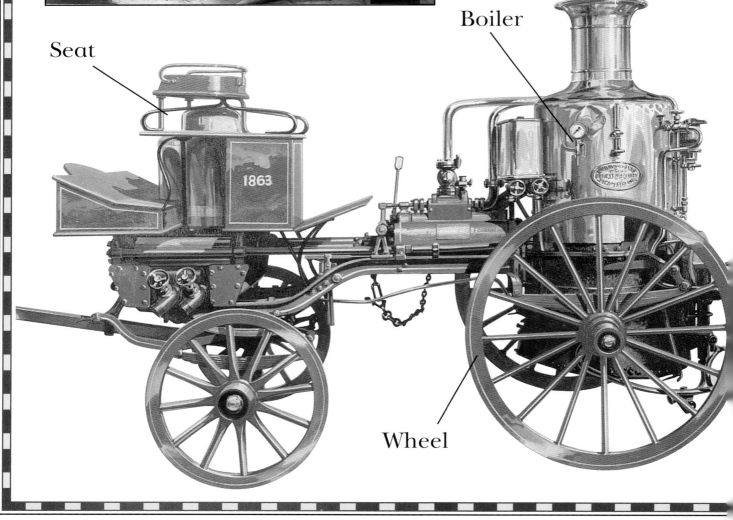

Boiler

Seat

1863

Wheel

all shapes and sizes.

Today's trucks

This tiny fire engine (*left*) carries ladders, hoses, and two firefighters. It can get to fires down very narrow streets.

This fire engine (*right*) is small. It works at an oil refinery and needs to get to a fire quickly. Normal trucks (*below*) are big because they have to carry lots of equipment.

Turntable
The ladder is attached to a turntable. This can spin the ladder in a complete circle. The end of the ladder can also move up and down.

Stabilizer
These special legs stop the fire truck from falling over when the ladder is used.

AERIAL LADDER
Sometimes, firefighters need to reach fires in high places. To do this they use a long ladder.

Ladder
When the truck has got to the fire, the ladder extends to reach the flames.

Rear cab
From here, a firefighter can steer the wheels at the back. This helps the fire truck to turn very tight corners.

Equipment stores
Firefighters need a lot of equipment to put out a fire. This fire truck has enough space under the ladder to store all the gear they use.

Hose
The ladder has a hose at the end of it. A firefighter can use this hose to put out fires in high places.

This fire truck has a very long ladder. It is as tall as 20 people standing on top of each other! There is also a cab where the firefighters can sit. Even though it is very long, this fire truck can drive down winding streets because its back can swing.

Firefighters can get

Ladder rescue

People can get trapped in tall burning buildings. To rescue them, firefighters climb up a long ladder and help the people back down to safety (*left*).

High hoses

The hose on the end of a ladder lets firefighters spray water at flames that are far beyond the range of hoses on the ground (*below*).

Dropping in

Sometimes, even the longest ladder is not long enough. If this happens, firefighters may have to climb down the side of a building to reach a blaze (*above*).

to very high places.

Platform

Firefighter standing on a platform

Going up...

This fire truck (*right*) does not have a ladder. Instead, it has a platform on the end of a long arm. This can reach as high as an aerial ladder (*see* page 9).

Cab

Stabilizer

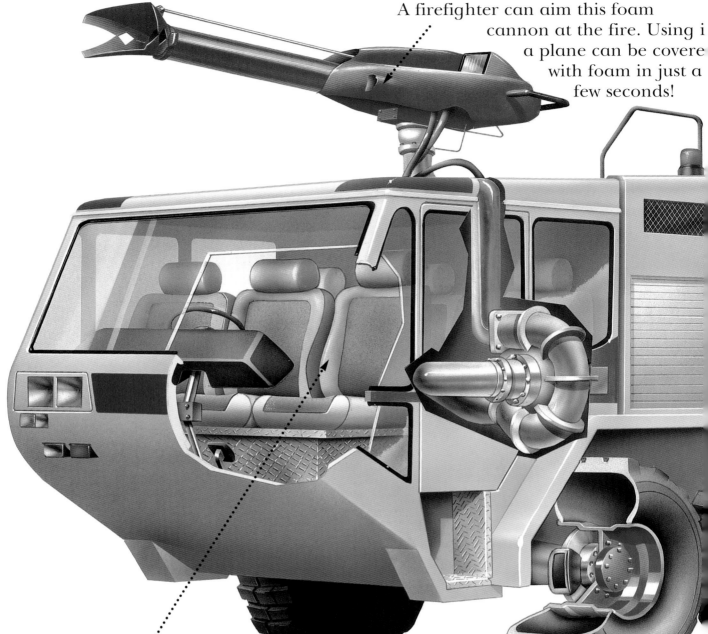

Foam cannon
A firefighter can aim this foam cannon at the fire. Using i a plane can be covere with foam in just a few seconds!

Cab
The big windows give the firefighters a good view of the fire. The cab also has bright lights to help them to see in the dark.

AIRPORT TRUCK

Fires at airports can be very dangerous. Disasters can happen in just a few seconds because aircraft fuel burns very easily.

Foam tank

Foam is stored in a huge tank inside the airport truck. From here, a powerful pump forces foam out through the foam cannon.

Engine

The engine is very powerful. It has to drive the truck at high speed and power the pump.

Equipment

The airport truck has equipment that the firefighters might need to rescue people from a burning plane. This includes ladders and breathing equipment.

When it arrives at a fire, the airport truck covers the blaze with a thick blanket of foam. Foam is used because water would not stop aircraft fuel from burning. The truck is always on alert, because planes are always landing at busy airports.

Different emergencies

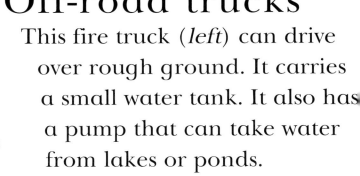

Off-road trucks

This fire truck (*left*) can drive over rough ground. It carries a small water tank. It also has a pump that can take water from lakes or ponds.

Rescue truck

Not all emergencies are fires. This truck (*right*) has a crane to lift heavy objects. It also carries equipment to rescue people trapped in cars or even underground.

Shine a light!

This fire truck (*left*) has very bright lights. These are attached to a pole that can be raised high above the truck. This helps firefighters to see during an emergency.

need different trucks.

Crane

Command cab

Some fires are very big and need many firefighters to put them out. To direct such operations, a fire chief uses a special truck (*below*). This has a cab at the rear that acts as a command center.

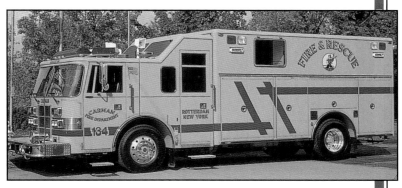

Stabilizer

Extra foam

For very big fires, extra foam may be needed. The foam carrier (*right*) carries enough spare foam to help put out the largest fires.

What it takes to

On standby

A lot of a firefighter's time is spent waiting for the next emergency. If the alarm sounds when they are eating (*left*), they have to leave their food.

Into action

Firefighters need to act quickly when the alarm sounds. Sometimes, they slide down a pole (*right*) to get to their fire trucks as quickly as possible. Every second counts!

Safe breathing

Firefighters protect themselves from smoke and fumes by wearing equipment (*left*) that gives them air to breathe.

be a firefighter.

Cleaning up

Sometimes, firefighters don't have to tackle a blaze. They may have to clean up some dangerous chemicals. To do this, they wear special suits (*left*).

Be prepared

After an emergency, firefighters have to clean and check all their equipment (*right*). They then get ready for the next alarm...

Cab
The front cab is equipped with sirens, flashing lights, and a radio. It can carry three firefighters and the driver.

Equipment
There are fire extinguishers and breathing equipment in the front cab. It also holds stretchers and a first-aid kit.

Tracks
Instead of wheels, this truck has tracks. These help it to drive over very rough ground.

TRACKED TRUCK
This truck is used to get to fires in hard-to-reach places. It can drive through a mudd field, and even travel through rivers!

18

Foam tank
The rear cab holds a large tank. This contains foam that the firefighters use to put out a blaze.

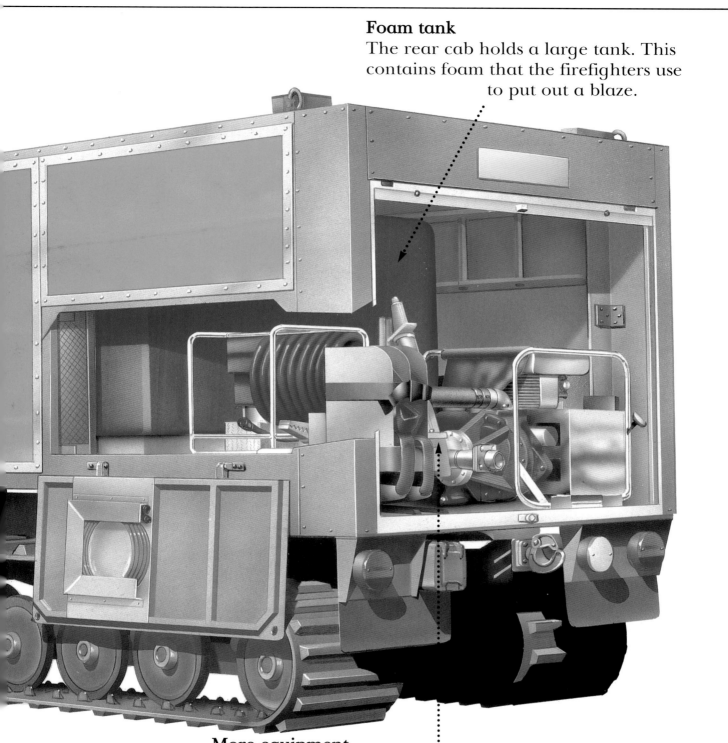

More equipment
The rear cab holds rescue equipment, ladders, a pump, and some hoses.

However, the ground may be too rough even for this truck. If this happens, it can be picked up and flown to a fire by helicopter.

Although they are small, the cabs of the truck can carry a team of firefighters and the equipment they need to tackle a blaze.

Fighting fires in

Guarding the tunnel

Specially built fire trucks (*right*) are used in the Channel Tunnel, which runs between England and France. These drive down a rescue tunnel to reach a fire on a train.

Fire suit

Very hot fires need special safety gear to fight them. This suit (*above left*) protects firefighters from high-temperature fires.

Oil-well fire

At an oil-well fire, firefighters put up barriers to protect themselves (*left*). When they stand behind them, they are shielded from the heat of the flames

strange places.

Fire marshal

Racing cars can catch fire easily because they carry lots of fuel. As a result, car races have their own special firefighters (*below*). If there is a fire, they will put out the flames and rescue the driver.

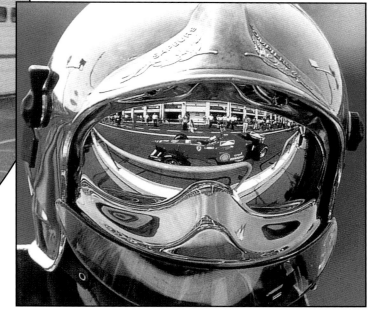

Robot fire fighter

This robot fire fighter (*right*) is used to get to fires that human firefighters couldn't reach. These could be in very small spaces or in places too dangerous for people.

Radar

The radar spins around and around. Fire tugs use radar to find other ships, especially ones in trouble.

Bridge

The captain of the fire tug stands on the bridge. This gives a good view around the tug and lets the captain direct the firefighting.

Crew's quarters

There are bunks for the crew below deck. Here, the crew can rest when they are going to, or coming from, a fire.

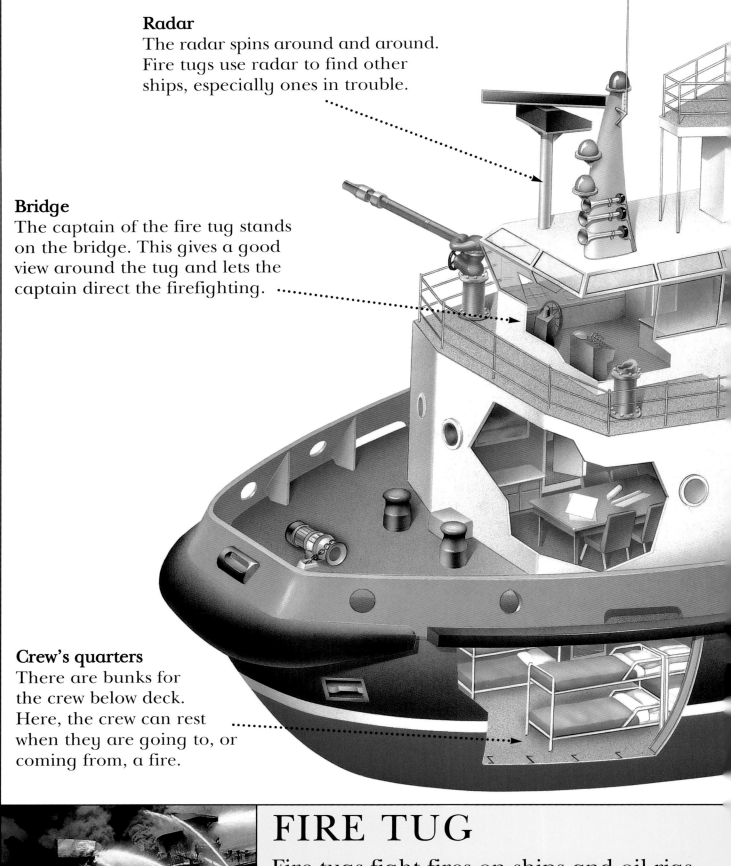

FIRE TUG

Fire tugs fight fires on ships and oil rigs. They also tackle blazes that are on land a ports, harbors, and along rivers.

22

Water cannons
The fire tug has several water cannons. These can be swiveled and moved up and down.

Lifeboat
The fire tug has its own lifeboat. The crew can lower it quickly into the water if the tug gets into trouble.

Engines
The fire tug has powerful engines. These push the boat through the roughest seas.

The captain guides the boat close to the fire. The tug then pumps seawater or river water out through its water cannons.

These throw out massive jets of water that spray over long distances – up to the length of a football field!

Fires at sea can be

Support at sea

This huge craft (*right*) is called an Emergency Support Vessel (ESV). It is used to fight serious fires on oil rigs. It has helicopters to rescue people and cranes to lift objects out of the water.

Crane

Water hose

Lifeboat

RESCUE-TOOLS
EMERGENCY
USE
ONLY

Fuel

Water cannons

The ESV is equipped with water cannons (*left*). These special hoses are similar to those on a fire tug (*see* pages 22-23).

very dangerous.

Oil-rig fires

Fires on oil rigs (*left*) are very fierce. This is because the oil and gas rushes up from the seabed very quickly. This makes the fire very difficult to put out.

Helicopter

Powerful jets

The huge jets of water from a fire tug's cannons show how powerful its pumps are (*right*).

Propeller

Coast guard

When a fire occurs on a small boat, the coast guard may respond to the alarm (*left*). They have fast boats that can rescue people before a blaze gets out of control.

Fuel tanks
The aircraft carries fuel in tanks that are in its wings.

Engine
This water bomber has four engines. They are powerful enough to lift the plane when it is carrying water.

Water tanks
Water is carried in huge tanks. These are carried in the water bomber's body.

Cabin
The flight crew sit in the cabin. Behind this are bunks where they can rest.

WATER BOMBER

A water bomber is an aircraft that can drop water on a fire. It is used to fight forest fires especially in areas that are hard to reach.

Lightweight

To keep the plane as light as possible, it is made from aluminum. This metal weighs very little.

Tail

The tail of the plane helps to make it stable in flight. The rear part of the tail is a rudder. This helps to steer the plane.

Hoses

Two huge hoses stick out of the rear of the plane. When the water bomber flies over a fire, the water is forced out of these hoses. The water tanks can be emptied in a few seconds!

The aircraft flies low over a fire. With one pass, the plane can spray water over a large area of burning woodland.

The water bomber then returns to its airfield. Here, it refills its tanks with more water, before flying back to fight the fire.

There are many ways

Jumping into fires

Some firefighters are trained to parachute close to forest fires (*left*). This is useful when they are needed in a hurry at fires that are hard to reach.

Beating fires

Firefighters often try to beat out a forest fire (*below*). This is a good way to fight fires where no water is available.

Starting fires

Some fires are started deliberately (*above*). By burning forest scrub in a controlled way, firefighters can prevent serious forest fires from spreading.

to fight forest fires.

Helicopters

Helicopters can hover over the site of a fire. They drop water from a bucket which they carry beneath (*right*).

Water bucket

Forest truck

Special trucks carry firefighters to forest fires (*right*). They are built to drive over rough ground.

Fantastic Facts

• The first organized fire brigade was in ancient Rome. The firefighters were equipped with hand pumps, ladders, buckets, and pickaxes. They also had blankets to protect them from heat.

• In 1982, a fire in Borneo lasted for 10 months. It was only put out when heavy rain started to fall.

• In the summer of 1988, a forest fire at Yellowstone National Park, Wyoming, burned about half the park's area. At one time, nearly 9,500 firefighters were used to tackle the blaze.

• Smoke kills more people than fire itself. This is why breathing equipment is so important in helping to fight fires and rescue people trapped in a blaze.

Glossary

Aerial ladder
A fire truck that can be steered from the rear as well as the front.

Breathing equipment
A device that supplies air to a face mask worn by firefighters. This lets them breathe in a smoke-filled room.

Coast guard
An organization that watches the coastline to prevent accidents and smuggling.

Emergency Support Vessel (ESV)
A huge, floating platform that is used to fight fires on oil rigs.

Siren
A device attached to a vehicle that makes a wailing sound. This warns people that firefighters are coming.

Track
A loop that runs around wheels, helping a vehicle over rough ground.

Turntable
The base on which the ladder rests. It allows it to turn in a circle.

Water cannon
A special device attached to a fire tug or ESV. It is used to point a jet of water at a fire.

Index

PHOTO CREDITS
Abbreviations; t-top, m-middle, b-bottom, r-right, l-left

Pages 4, 10b, 16 both, 17t, 20m, 28b & 29b – Shout Pictures.
6t – Hulton Getty Collection. 7tl – Rex Features. 7tr, 11, 14 both, 15b & 18 – Angloco Ltd. 7b, 8 & 15m – Pierce Manufacturing. 10t, 24 & 25m – Eye Ubiquitous. 10m, 12, 20b, 20-21, 21b, 22, 25t & b, 26, 28t & 28-29 – Frank Spooner Pictures. 16b – Spectrum Color Library. 17b – Science Photo Library. 21m – Empics.

LOOK INSIDE MACHINES

SPACE VEHICLES

JON RICHARDS

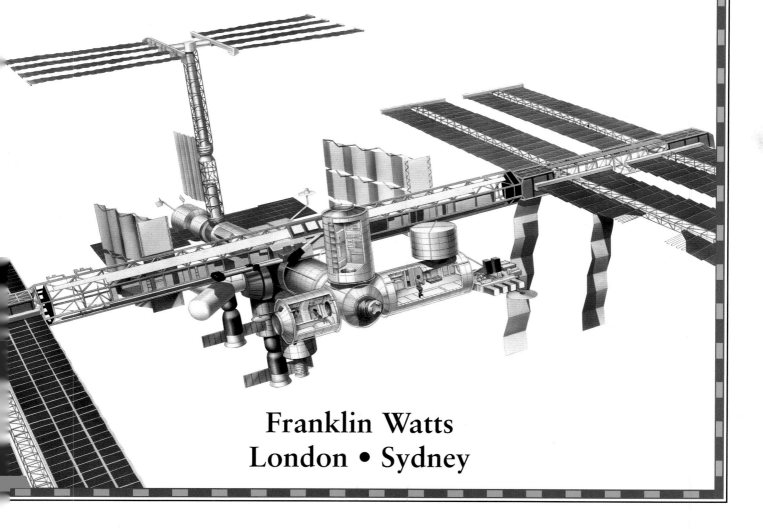

Franklin Watts
London • Sydney

CONTENTS

INTRODUCTION

It is less than fifty years since we sent the first object out into space. Since then, robot probes have been to nearly every planet in our solar system — a couple have left it altogether and are traveling out to the stars. We have also sent people out of the earth's atmosphere. In specially made space vehicles, they have even been to the moon and back!

Communications

These antennae on the front of the space vehicle sent information to mission control (*see* page 11).

Heat shield

This protected the capsule and stopped it from burning up when it reentered the atmosphere.

Instrument panel

In front of the cosmonaut was a panel of instruments that told him how the space vehicle was performing.

Reentry vehicle

After orbiting the earth, the capsule at the front of the space vehicle broke off and returned to Earth with the cosmonaut.

VOSTOK 1

On April 12, 1961, Yuri A. Gagarin, a Russia cosmonaut, became the first person to leave the earth and go into space.

Life-support bottles
These small, ball-shaped containers held the gas that allowed the cosmonaut to breathe while he was in space.

Equipment module
This part of the space vehicle had small rockets that controlled the spacecraft in space.

He traveled in a spacecraft called *Vostok 1*. This was a small metal vehicle that was fitted to the top of a rocket.

After orbiting, or going around, the earth, he reentered the atmosphere and parachuted safely to the ground.

Many attempts were

Explosive

Fuel
tank

Flying bombs
These rockets (*left*) were used toward the end of World War II. They were called V2s. They soared up to the edge of space before diving down onto a target and exploding.

Rocket
engine

Sputnik
The first object sent into space was a small silver ball called *Sputnik 1* (*left*). It was launched in October 1957. The next month a second spacecraft, *Sputnik 2*, was sent into space. This time it carried a living thing — a small dog named Laika (*right*).

made to reach space.

Probing the moon

Many probes have been sent to study the moon. One spacecraft, *Luna 16* (*right*), was sent in September 1970. It gathered samples of rock using a drill and brought them back to Earth.

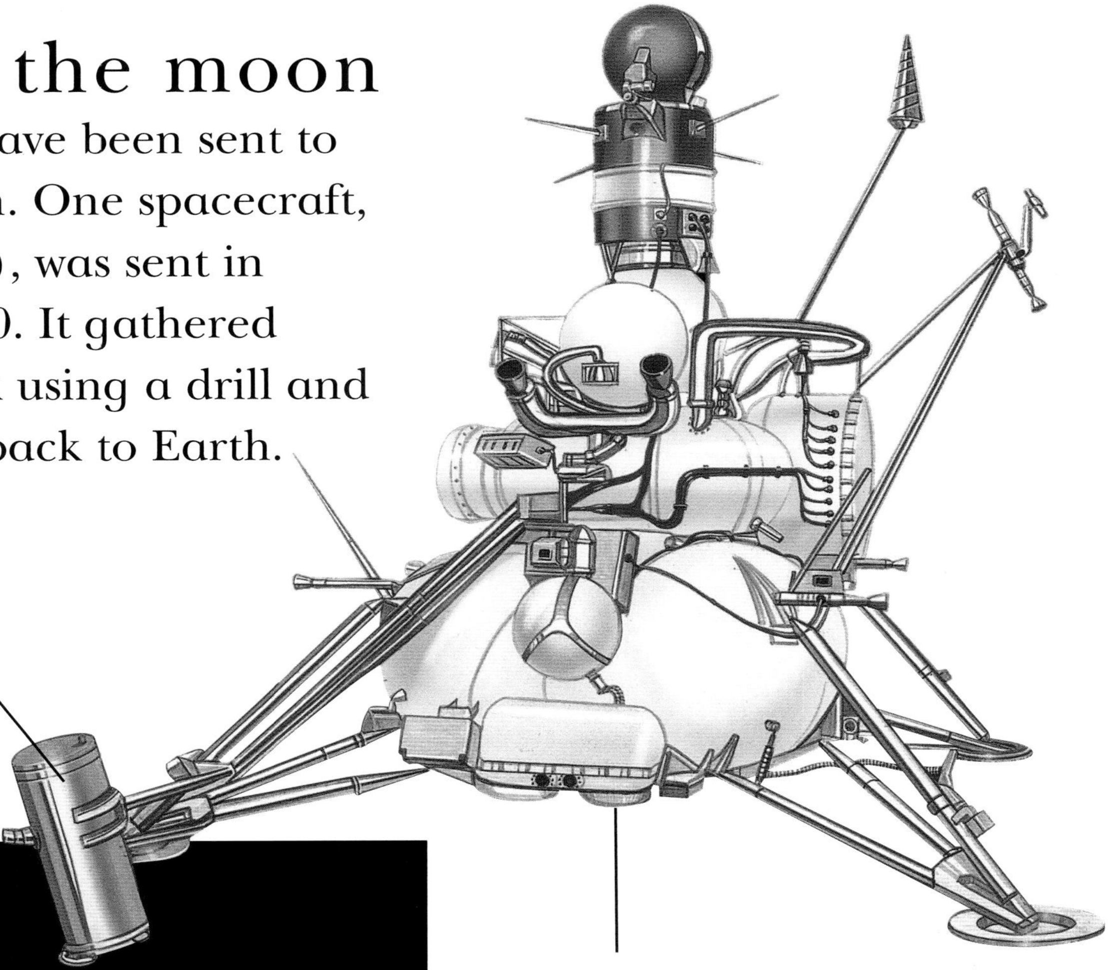

Drill

Rocket engine

Gemini

Some of the earliest U.S. astronauts were carried into space in *Gemini* space vehicles (*left*). These capsules could carry two astronauts at a time.

First stage
The first stage of the *Saturn 5* had five powerful engines that blasted the rocket clear of the launch pad (*see* page 14).

Fuel tanks
Inside each of the stages were huge tanks of fuel and oxygen. These were mixed in the rocket engines and burned to produce the thrust.

Third stage
The third and final stage of the *Saturn 5* held the modules that carried the astronauts to the moon.

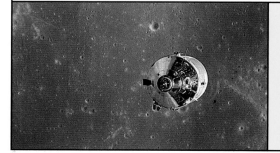

SATURN 5

One of the most powerful rockets ever buil was the *Saturn 5*. This mighty space vehicle carried astronauts to the moon.

Second stage

The first stage broke away from the rocket when the fuel in its tanks was used up. The rockets in the second stage were then ignited.

Escape rocket

In an emergency, this would carry the astronauts clear of any danger.

Moon modules

These small modules sat on top of the *Saturn 5* rocket. The astronauts traveled to the moon inside them (*see* pages 12-13).

t had three sets of rocket ngines. These were housed in hree separate parts, called tages (*see* page 14).

The *Saturn 5* rocket was very long. If it had been put on its side it would have stretched the length of a football field.

9

Rockets are used to

Firing rockets

The rocket sits silently on the launch pad as the seconds tick down to the launch. Then, when the countdown has finished, the engines ignite (*left*) and push the rocket into the air. BLAST OFF!

Rocket shapes

Rockets have been built in many different shapes and sizes (*right*). Today, they can carry huge satellites into orbit, or send probes out to the planets.

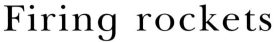

lift things into space.

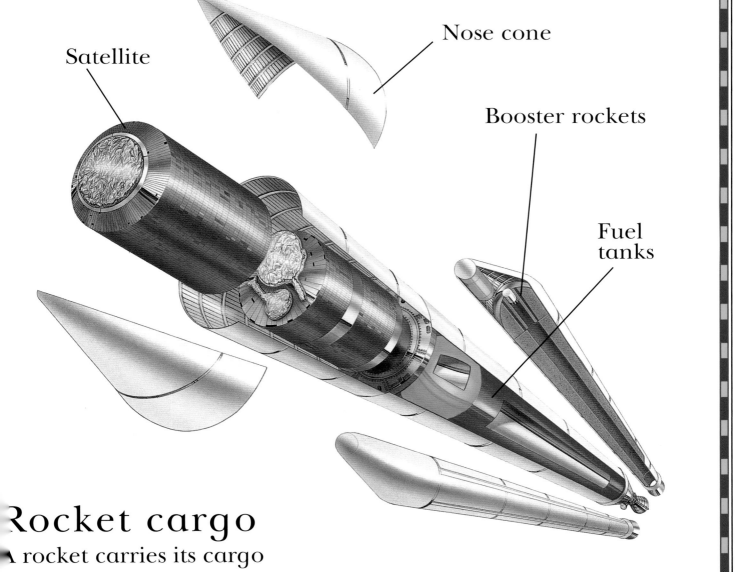

Satellite

Nose cone

Booster rockets

Fuel tanks

Rocket cargo

A rocket carries its cargo inside its nose cone (*above*). This cargo could be one or two satellites. As it flies through the atmosphere and space, the rocket is guided and watched from mission control (*right*).

Command module
This is where the astronauts sat during blast-off.

Service module
The service module held the fuel and life-support systems for the mission to the moon.

Control engines
On the side of each module were small rocket engines. These were used to steer the vehicle through space.

MOON MODULES
The U.S. astronauts traveled to the moon inside three space vehicles that were joined together for most of the journey.

Lunar module
Once on the moon, the astronauts left the lunar module to explore the surface.

Leaving the moon
This rocket blasted the astronauts clear of the moon's surface and up to the orbiting modules.

Legs
When the mission was completed on the surface, the top half of the lunar module blasted clear, leaving the legs on the moon.

These three space vehicles were called the command module, the service module, and the lunar module.

The lunar module carried two astronauts down to the moon, while the third astronaut stayed in orbit around the moon.

What it took to put

Blast off

At the end of the countdown, the engines at the the bottom of the *Saturn 5* were ignited. The force from the burning gases pushed the rocket into the atmosphere and toward the moon (*left*).

Stages

After it had broken away from the *Saturn 5* (*left*), each stage of the rocket fell back to Earth and burned up in the upper atmosphere.

Moon walk

After they landed on the moon, the astronauts put on special suits to walk on the surface (*left*). Here they collected rocks and carried out experiments.

Radio antenna

Camera

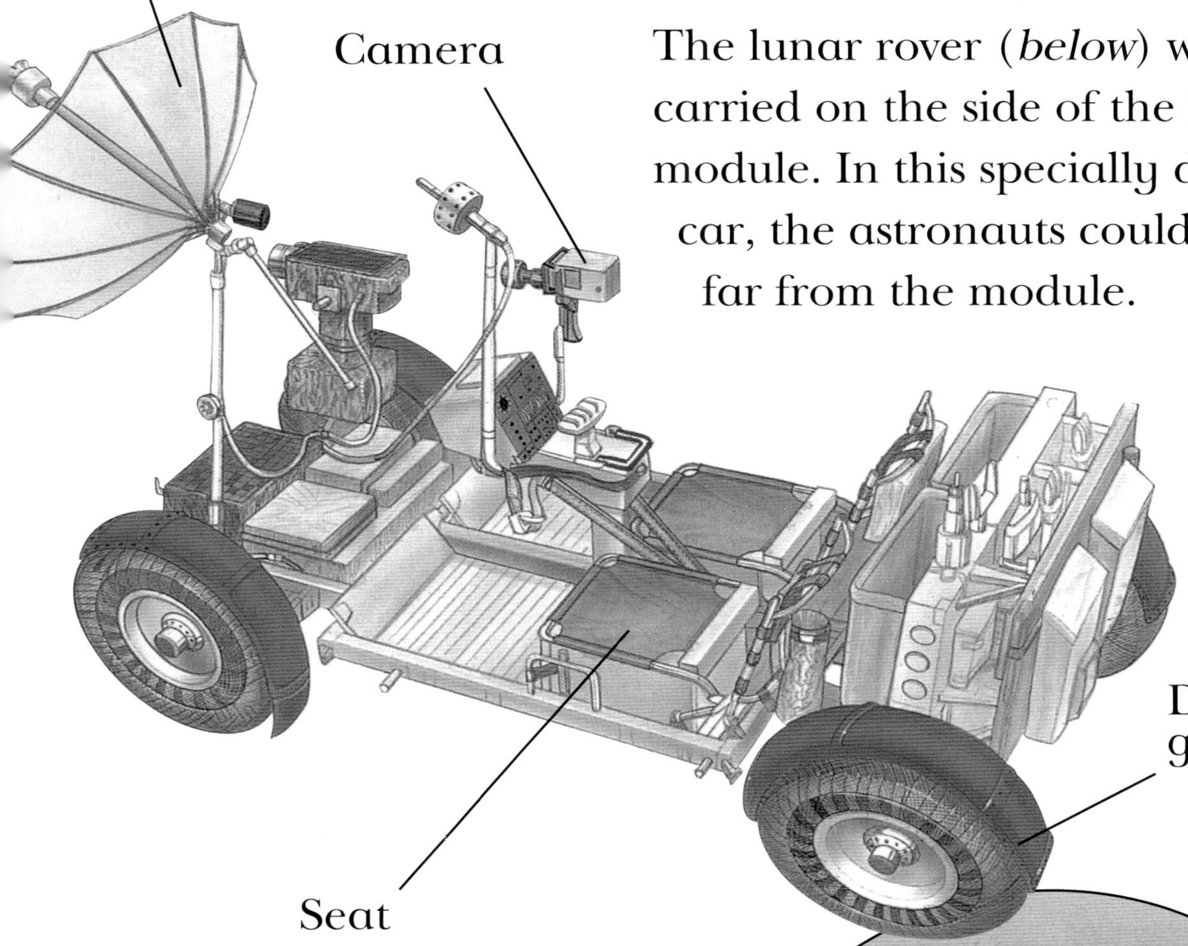

Lunar rover

The lunar rover (*below*) was carried on the side of the lunar module. In this specially designed car, the astronauts could drive far from the module.

Dust guard

Seat

Splash down

The astronauts returned to Earth inside the command module. After it entered the Earth's atmosphere, several parachutes opened to slow the module down. It finally landed in the Pacific Ocean (*right*).

What it takes to

Survival training

Astronauts need survival training in case they do not land where they had planned. They could land in the middle of a huge forest or in the wrong part of the sea (*left*).

Underwater

To cope with being weightless, astronauts practice in swimming pools (*right*). Here they can float freely — just like being in space.

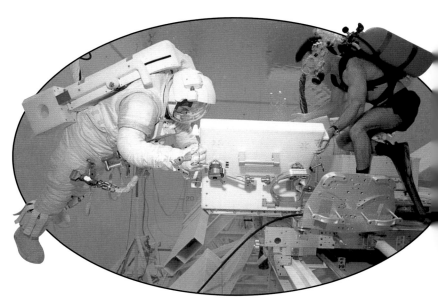

Floating freely

Astronauts can use a plane to practice being weightless. This flies in a special way that makes those people inside it float freely (*left*). It only lasts a short time, but it can still make people feel ill!

be an astronaut.

Visor

Camera

Space suit

Controls

Rocket pack

This rocket pack (*left*) was used by astronauts to fly around without being attached to their spacecraft. It had an air supply to let the astronaut breathe and rockets to push the astronaut around in space.

Locked up

When the first astronauts came back from the moon they were put in special chambers (*right*). Scientists thought that they might infect humans with germs that might live on the moon.

17

Rocket engines
The shuttle has three main engines.
These help to push the spacecraft into
the atmosphere along with the powerful
rocket boosters (*see* pages 20-21).

Wings
The shuttle uses
wings to glide
through the air
after it reenters
the atmosphere.

SPACE SHUTTLE

In 1981 the space shuttle *Columbia*
blasted off to become the world's first
reusable space vehicle.

Cargo bay

The shuttle has cargo doors that open to reveal the cargo bay. Here satellites can be carried into orbit or rescued and brought back to Earth for repair.

Robot arm

The shuttle is fitted with a special robot arm. Astronauts control the arm and use it to launch satellites or bring them into the cargo bay.

Crew's quarters

Up to eight astronauts can live and work in the shuttle's small quarters. These are found behind and beneath the flight deck.

Landing gear

For much of the mission these wheels are folded into the shuttle's nose and wings. Like the wheels of a plane, they are lowered as the shuttle glides in to land.

Since then the space shuttles have been used in a huge variety of ways. They have carried satellites into orbit, repaired broken satellites, and docked with space stations. They have also carried out studies into how we could live in space.

The space shuttle does

Liftoff

When the space shuttle blasts off it is fitted to two rocket boosters and a big fuel tank (*left*). The boosters are released soon after launch. They parachute back to Earth and are used in a later mission.

Fixing satellites

Sometimes satellites may need to be repaired. The shuttle can either bring them back down to Earth, or astronauts can fix them while they are still in space (*right*).

many different jobs.

Docking

The Russian space station, *Mir* (*left*) served 15 years in orbit. Previous shuttle missions to Mir have allowed astronauts to practice for the building of a future space station (*see* pages 26-27). Mir was finally retired in 2001

Landing

After the shuttle has reentered Earth's atmosphere, it glides down to land at a special airstrip that is near its launch pad (*right*).

Protective shell
When it entered the atmosphere, the lander was protected by a special shell. This was dropped before the lander touched down.

Communications
Small antennae on the spacecraft kept it in touch with Earth. They also sent back information and any pictures taken by the probe.

Fuel tanks
Fuel to power the space probe's small rocket engines was stored in tanks inside the spacecraft.

Lander
When *Viking* reached Mars, the lander was released. It entered the atmosphere and parachuted to the ground. Before it touched down, small rockets fired to slow it even more, and let it land very gently.

Solar panels
These convert sunlight into electricity to supply the probe with power during its mission.

VIKING PROBES

In 1976, two probes were sent to Mars. Both called *Viking*, they were each made up of two parts. One part of each probe landed on the planet's surface. The other part stayed in orbit around Mars and sent information back to Earth. Once on the surface, the two landers took many pictures of the landscape. They were also fitted with special tools. These were used to carry out experiments to study the Martian rocks and soil.

Many probes have

Galileo

Galileo (*right*) traveled to the largest planet in the solar system, Jupiter. It looked at Jupiter's moons and sent a tiny probe into the atmosphere of the giant planet.

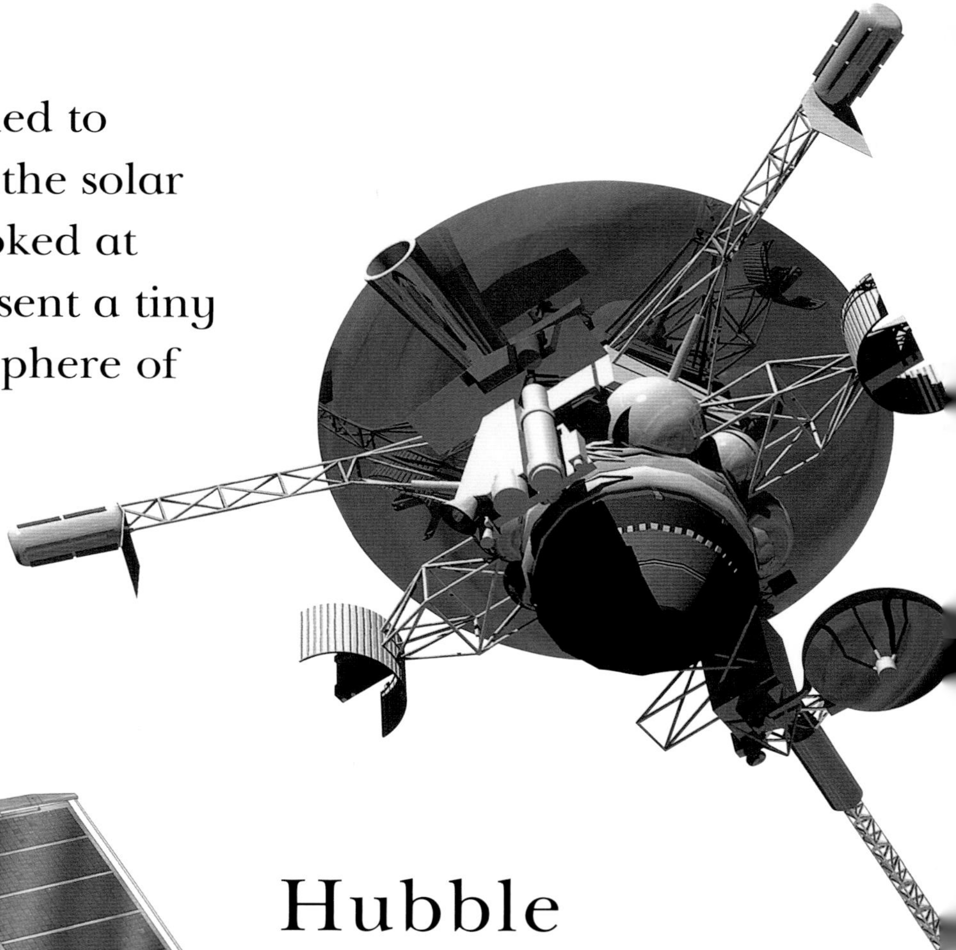

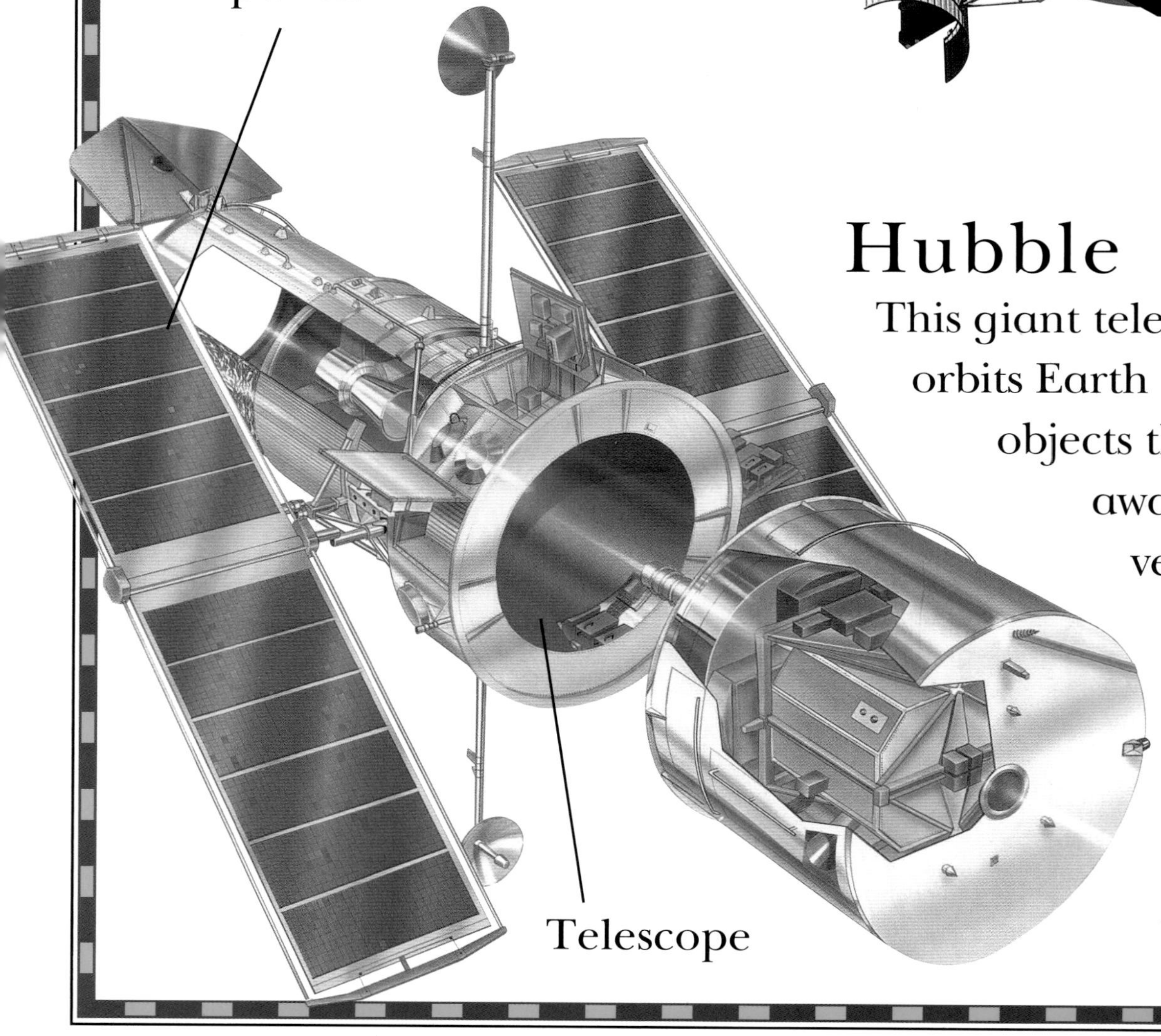

Solar panels

Hubble

This giant telescope (*left*) orbits Earth looking at objects that are very far away. It has been very useful in helping us to understand what happened just after the universe was formed.

Telescope

been sent into space.

Pathfinder

Pathfinder landed on Mars in 1997. It carried a robot vehicle called *Sojourner* (*right*). This explored the area around the lander and examined rocks and soil on the surface.

Giotto

Halley's Comet flies past Earth every 76 years. In 1986 a probe called *Giotto* (*left*) was sent to travel into the comet's tail and take pictures of the comet's center.

Laboratories
Inside these parts of the space station astronauts will carry out many experiments.

Docking
When spaceships come up from Earth, they will dock at a special port on the space station.

Escape capsule
In an emergency the astronauts can leave the space station in a special capsule and return safely to Earth.

SPACE STATION
The International Space Station will be built by countries from all over the world, including the U.S.A., Russia, and Japan.

26

Structure

The space station will be too big to take into space in one piece. Instead, parts will be carried up in stages and put together while in orbit.

Solar panels

These will need to be massive to supply the space station with all the energy it will use.

Living quarters

Although the living quarters are small, seven astronauts will be able to live in them.

It will orbit high above Earth, and people will live and work inside. It will also show how well humans can live in space.

In the future, the astronauts may be carried up to the space station by the next generation of space shuttles.

Eating

Because everything is weightless in space, astronauts eat food from specially made containers and tubes (*above*). Otherwise the food would float around in a gooey mess!

Exercise

Because they can float around in space without any effort, astronauts need to exercise (*right*). If they did not their muscles would waste away and they would have trouble walking when they returned to Earth.

a lot of problems.

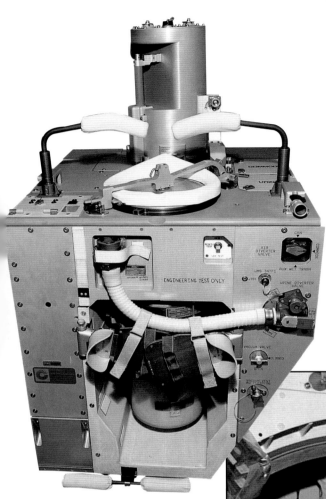

Space toilet

Going to the bathroom in space can cause problems! To overcome this scientists have built a special toilet (*left*) to let astronauts go without causing a mess.

Washing

Specially designed washing facilities help astronauts keep themselves clean — without getting the rest of the spacecraft wet (*right*)!

Fantastic facts

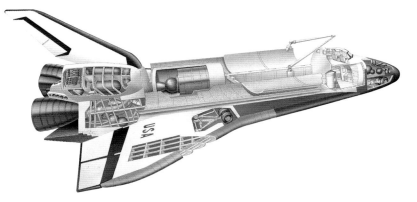

• The most powerful rocket ever built was the Russian NI booster. Launched in 1969, it exploded just 70 seconds after blast-off.

• The space probe *Pioneer 10* is currently the farthest artificial object sent into space. It passed beyond the orbit of Pluto in 1986 and is now nearly 6 billion miles (10 billion km) away from Earth.

• The Hubble Space Telescope is the largest telescope in space. It weighs more than two fully grown elephants!

• The *Pathfinder* probe that landed on Mars in 1997 was fitted with the most powerful computer to go into space. This was capable of handling 22 million instructions every second!

LOOK INSIDE MACHINES

TRAINS

JON RICHARDS

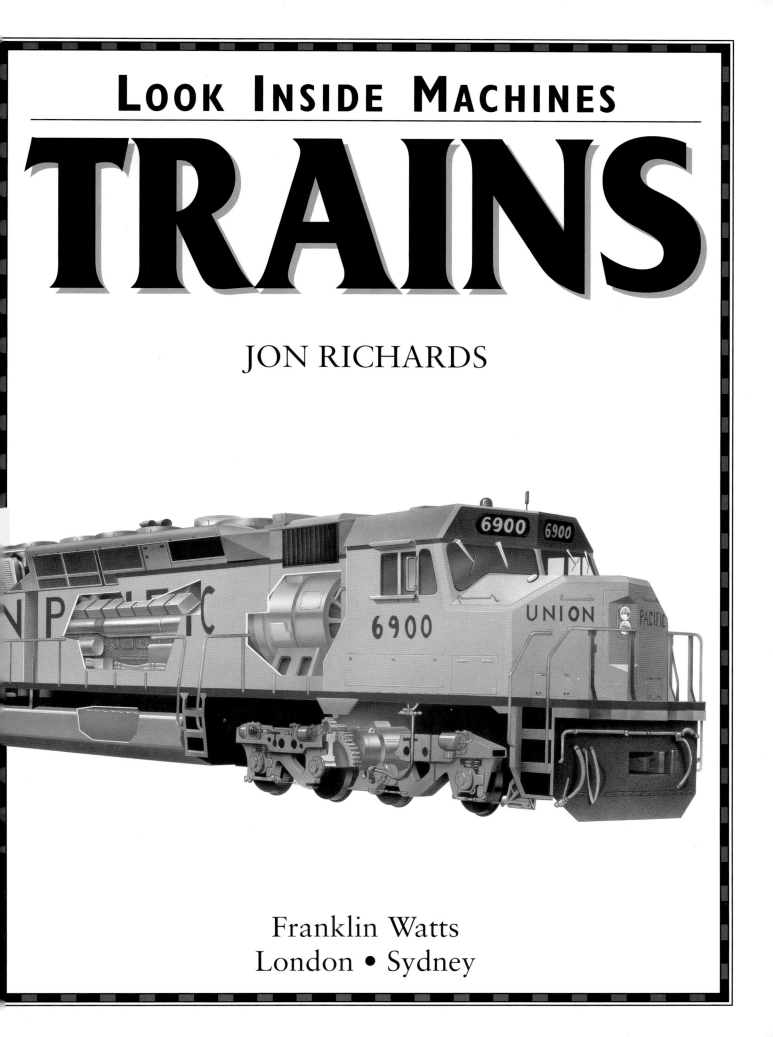

Franklin Watts
London • Sydney

© Aladdin Books Ltd

Designed and produced by Aladdin Books Ltd

Editor
Simon Beecroft
Consultant
Tony Hall-Patch
Design
David West
Children's Book Design
Designer
Robert Perry
Illustrators
Simon Tegg & Ross Watton
Picture Research
Brooks Krikler Research

CONTENTS

INTRODUCTION

Before the arrival of cars and trucks, we used trains to travel from place to place. We still use trains to get about, or to carry large loads of freight. But the puffing steam engines that once pulled the trains have been replaced by powerful diesel engines and very fast electric locomotives. Today, trains carry goods and people all over the world — some even run beneath our feet!

Tender
The small car behind the locomotive was called the tender. It carried the fuel for the fire and spare water for the locomotive.

Driver's cab
The driver's area on this locomotive was covered by a cab. This cab protected the drivers from the sun, the wind, and the rain.

Driving wheels
These huge wheels at the back of the locomotive drove the train along. They could be as tall as an adult!

EARLY STEAM TRAIN
This type of locomotive was used to pull passenger and freight trains during the early days of the American railroad.

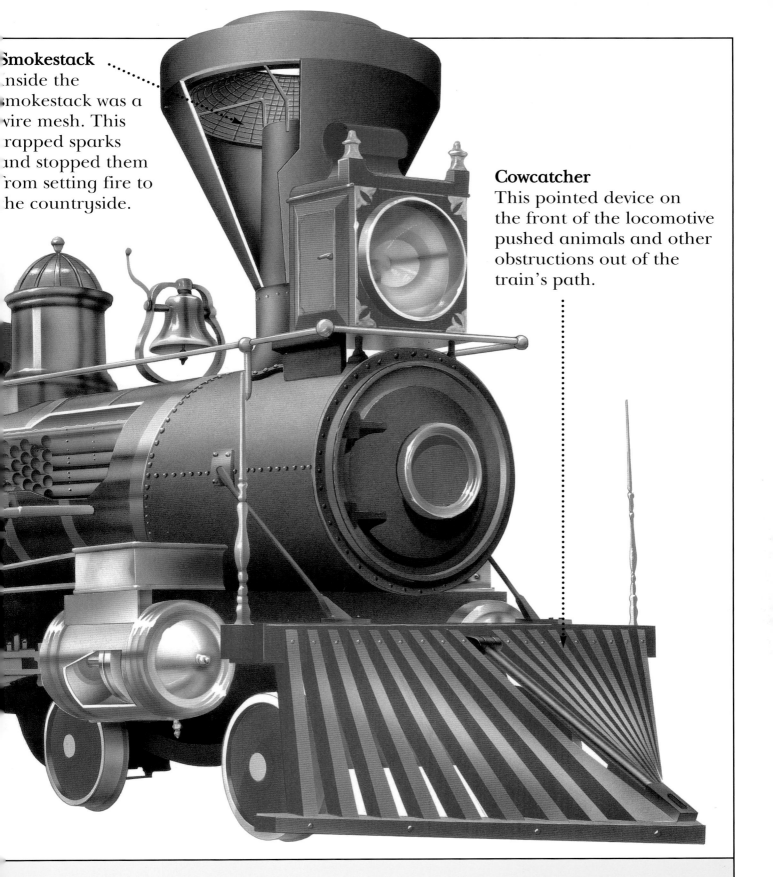

Smokestack
Inside the smokestack was a wire mesh. This trapped sparks and stopped them from setting fire to the countryside.

Cowcatcher
This pointed device on the front of the locomotive pushed animals and other obstructions out of the train's path.

It was called the 4-4-0 because it had four wheels at the front attached to a center pin and four large driving wheels at the rear. It also had a "cowcatcher" on the front and a large, bell-shaped chimney called a smokestack.

It takes a lot of work

Crossing a continent

The first railroad to run across an entire continent was built in the United States. Two companies started building from opposite coasts. They met in the mountains of Utah in 1869 (*right*).

Bridges

Sometimes, railroads come across large obstacles such as lakes or rivers. To cross them, railroad builders construct bridges. These can be made from metal, stone, or even wood. This bridge (*below*) crosses the Forth River in Scotland.

to build a railroad.

Digging Tunnels

Another way to cross lakes and rivers and even mountains is by digging tunnels beneath or through them. This picture (*below*) shows the building of the world's longest rail tunnel. It runs under the sea between two islands in Japan.

Beating a path

If a railroad has to run through a forest, a path is cut through the trees (*left*). The wood from the cut-down trees can be used to build the tracks.

Chimney
The chimney at the front carries the heated air and smoke out of the locomotive.

Leading truck
The front four wheels are attached to a center pin, which allows the truck to swivel when the train takes curves in the track.

Pistons and connecting rods
Pressure from the steam pushes the pistons backward and forward. The pistons move the connecting rods that turn the wheels.

THE FLYING SCOTSMAN

The *Flying Scotsman* pulled passenger trains between England and Scotland beginning in 1922. Because it carried a spare crew and

Boiler

Tubes carry heated air from the firebox through the boiler. This heats the water inside the boiler until the water becomes steam — just like a huge kettle!

Firebox

Coal from the tender is shoveled into the firebox. Here, it is burned to heat the water in the boiler.

Water scoop

Rather than stop to collect fresh water, a scoop under the tender picks up water from a trough on the track as the train goes along!

picked up fresh supplies on the move, the *Flying Scotsman* could do the 393-mile (633-km) journey without stopping. Although steam trains are no longer used for everyday train travel in Britain, the *Flying Scotsman* still pulls the occasional special train.

Passengers on trains

Sleeping well

Many trains that travel through the night are fitted with sleeping compartments. In these, beds can be folded down to give passengers a good night's sleep (*left*).

Royal trains

When royalty use trains to travel from place to place, they do so in the utmost luxury. This passenger car (*below*) was used by Queen Victoria. The insides look more like a hotel than a railroad car!

can travel in luxury.

Freshen up

On the most luxurious train journeys, compartments may even have bathrooms (*right*). These help the passengers keep themselves clean.

Dining in style

Passengers on board some trains are treated to the best food. This is served at the tables by waiters (*below*).

Diesel engine
The Centennial locomotive has
two powerful diesel engines to
turn the electrical generators.
Together, these engines are
as powerful as 60 cars.

Quick starter
The crew on old steam trains
need time to light a fire and heat
the water in the boiler to make
steam. A diesel-electric locomotive
can be started a lot more quickly.

DIESEL-ELECTRIC
Diesel-electric locomotives use both diesel
engines and electric motors to power them.
This locomotive is the most powerful diesel-

Generators

When the generators are turned by the diesel engines, they produce electricity. This electricity powers the electric motors found in the trucks.

Coupler

Special couplers at the front and rear of the locomotive link it to the rest of the train.

6900 6900

6900

UNION PACIFIC

Power unit

Each truck on this locomotive has eight wheels as well as the electric motors that turn them.

electric locomotive ever built. It is called a Centennial class locomotive, and was built for the 100th birthday of the Union Pacific Railroad company. Centennial locomotives were used to pull very long freight trains across the United States.

Not every train is

Big Boy

This locomotive (*above* and *below*) was the largest steam engine ever built. It was so long that it had to bend in the middle to get around corners. It was built to pull freight trains and it could pull a load that weighed the same as 2,000 elephants!

built to carry people.

Loading up

This freight train (*left*) has wagons that are filled with rocks that have been dug up from the ground. Some freight trains have flat cars to carry containers. Others have special cars that can carry automobiles.

Long trains

Freight trains are very long to carry as much cargo as possible (*above*). The longest freight train was 4.5 miles (7.3 km) long. It had 660 cars and needed 16 locomotives to pull it!

What it takes to

Fierce fire

Steam trains need a very hot fire to heat the water to make the steam. Here (*left*), the stoker is shoveling coal into the firebox to keep the fire burning fiercely.

Modern trains

Today, train drivers don't need to shovel coal to drive the train. Instead, they sit in a cab at the front of the train (*right*), controlling the train's speed.

drive a locomotive.

Come together

To make a long train, the wagons are joined together by hooks on their fronts and backs. These hooks are called couplers (*see* page 13). When the wagons are ready, a locomotive is added to pull the train along (*left*).

n control

A railroad system is controlled by computers from a central control room (*right*). Here, controllers can check on the progress of trains and make sure that they are traveling in the right direction.

Driver's cab
From here, the driver controls the direction of the train, how quickly it accelerates, as well as the brakes that stop the train.

Go faster
To help the train go as quickly as possible, it has a pointed shape. This outline lets it travel through the air with the least effort.

A smooth ride
These pistons and springs make sure that the train rides smoothly over the tracks.

TGV

The TGV (Train à Grande Vitesse) is the world's fastest electric train and pulls passenger services throughout

Power lines
The cables that carry the electricity are supported by strong metal posts.

Pantograph
The TGV collects electricity using a special arm called a pantograph. This arm bends to keep it in contact with the power lines at all times.

Transformer
This converts the electricity that the pantograph collects into electricity that the locomotive can use to turn its wheels.

France. It can fly along the track at a breathtaking 186 mph (299 km/h) It is powered by electricity that it collects from power lines that run above the track.

Some trains are built

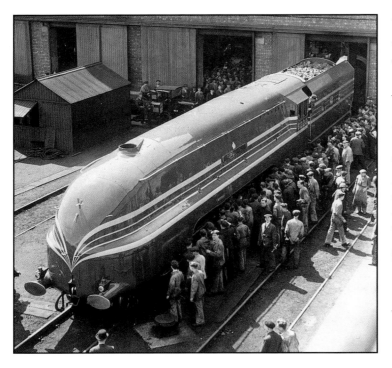

Fast steam

This steam train (*left*) was used in Britain during the 1930s. It was called a Coronation class locomotive. Its specially shaped body helped it to reach a top speed of 114 mph (184 km/h)! This was very fast for the time.

A speeding bullet

These trains (*below*) carry people in Japan. They were so fast when they were first used in 1964 that they were called "bullet" trains.

to travel very quickly.

European speed
This high-speed train (*above*) travels through Europe.
It is called ICE, which is short for Inter-City Express,
and it can zoom along at 206 mph (330 km/h).

Eurostar
This train (*right*) goes between
London and the cities
of Paris and Brussels.
It travels through the
Channel Tunnel
that runs under the
English Channel.
It can cruise along
at 180 mph (290 km/h).

SUBWAY TRAIN

Many cities around the world have large systems of underground railroads, or subways. The trains that run through these

Hanging around
This subway train is fitted with handles. People can hold on to these for support when they are standing up during their train journey.

Take a seat
Passengers can sit down in seats that are lined up along either side of the train's cars.

Sliding doors
The doors on this subway train slide open automatically once the train has stopped at a station.

tunnels are no longer powered by steam or diesel because the fumes and smoke remained in the underground tunnels.

Instead, they are powered by electricity, and pick up their power through "live" rails that run along the floor.

Driver's controls
One of the driver's controls is called a "dead-man's handle." If the driver lets go of this for any reason the brakes come on automatically and the train stops.

"Live" rails
Two of the four rails that this train runs on are called "live" rails. They carry the electricity that powers the train.

Some trains carry

Early subways

The first underground railroad ran beneath the streets of London (*above*). Since those early days, the London system has grown and now uses electric trains instead of the early steam locomotives. It has 253 miles (408 km) of track and 275 stations. Many of these stations are a maze of platforms, escalators, and tunnels (*right*).

Escalators

Platforms

people underground.

Beneath the waves

The Channel Tunnel under the English Channel (*see* page 21) consists of two main tunnels and a central service tunnel (*right*). There are also emergency access tunnels running between them to let passengers escape from an accident.

Service tunnel

Emergency access tunnel

Automatic pilot

This train (*left*), first installed in 1927, runs beneath London without a driver. It is still used by the Royal Mail service to carry mail between sorting post offices.

Putting on the brakes

A maglev train doesn't have any brakes like a normal train. Instead, the force of the magnets under the train is reversed to bring it to a stop.

Passenger comfort

Because a maglev train does not run on rails, passengers enjoy a smoother and quieter ride than the ride on a normal train.

Zooming along

Maglev trains can reach very high speeds because they do not have to scrape along metal rails. Some of them can reach 315 mph (500 km/h)!

MAGLEV TRAIN

Instead of running on rails, a maglev (short for magnetic levitation) train actually floats above the ground!

Magnets

The magnets that make a maglev train float are found on top of the track and along the bottom of the train.

Keep it on track

Sets of magnets in the walls of the maglev track guide the train along the route as it moves.

Hovering

When it is running, the body of the maglev train will float just $7/16$ inches (10 mm) above the track.

Special magnets run along the track and the train. An electronic control system keeps the vehicle levitating at a constant distance of 10 mm from its track guideway. The propulsion and braking systems are based on a rotating electric motor.

Some trains come

Mountain trains

Some trains run up the sides of mountains (*right*). To help them climb the steep slopes they have toothed wheels that pull the train up special middle rails.

Plane or train?

This experimental train (*right*) was pushed along by a huge spinning propeller. It could zoom along a monorail at 140 mph (220 km/h).

in unusual shapes.

City trains

Special short trains, or trams, run along tracks through the middle of some towns and cities (*right*). They help to reduce traffic congestion and pollution.

Monorail

Instead of running on two rails, some trains only use one rail. This one (*below*) travels on top of the rail — others may hang beneath it. These trains are called monorails.

Fantastic Facts

• The fastest steam locomotive in the world is called the *Mallard*. In 1938, it reached a speed of 125 mph (201 km/h) down Stoke Bank in the United Kingdom.

• The fastest vehicle ever run on a rail track was a rocket-powered sled. It reached a speed of 6,121 mph (9,851 km/h), or eight times the speed of sound. No one was on it at the time!

• The busiest underground railroad system in the world is the Greater Moscow Metro in Russia. It handles about 3.3 billion people every year!

• The United States has the greatest length of railroad track in the world. It has a staggering 138,666 miles (223,155 km) of railroad!

Train words

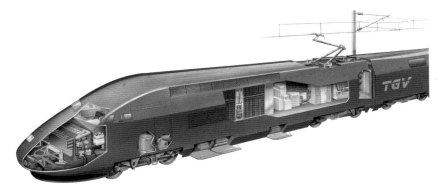

Boiler
The drumlike container on a steam locomotive where the water is heated and turned into steam.

Connecting rods
The rods that link the pistons to the wheels.

Cowcatcher
A pointed object on the front of a locomotive. It is used to push obstructions out of the train's path.

Firebox
Part of a steam locomotive where the fire is lit to heat the water in the boiler.

Locomotive
A self-propelling vehicle that is used to pull a train. It can be powered by steam, diesel, or electricity.

Stoking
Shoveling wood or coal into the firebox to fuel the fire.

Tender
The small wagon pulled behind the locomotive. It carries the fuel and water that the locomotive needs.

Truck
A wheeled trolley fitted to the bottom of a wagon or locomotive.

Index

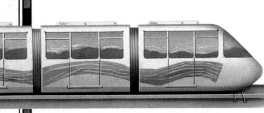

PHOTO CREDITS
Abbreviations: t-top, m-middle, b-bottom, r-right, l-left, c-center.

Pages 4, 7b, & 17t – Corbis. 6-7, 8, 20t, 24, 25, & 28 – Hulton Getty Collection. 7m, 10, 11 both, 16 both, 18, 21 both, 26, & 29 both – Frank Spooner Pictures. 12, 14 both, 17b, & 20b – Solution Pictures. 22 – Paul Nightingale.